All the world's a st

M R. PUNCH came to Weymouth in
stayed there ever since. He took his place on the beach among
the minstrels, pierrots and concert parties, outlasting every one
of them.

This book traces the performing lives of Weymouth's Punch
& Judy men – in particular the half-century reign of Frank Edmonds.
It tells how Punch and Pierrot travelled from Italy through France
and into England. It is the first account of their origins for more
than twenty years, and the only one to explore them through the
entertainment history of a single resort.

Weymouth would never have developed into a major resort were it not
for King George III, who holidayed in the town for sixteen years:
attending the little Theatre Royal on the Esplanade, bathing in the
sea and taking the waters in the little spas which ringed the town.
For without water, too, there would be no Weymouth.

The book is also a celebration of Weymouth, a unique place in the
history of the seaside and of popular entertainment, and in literary life.

Frank Edmonds with Dog Toby and Punch & Judy.

OPPOSITE: *Frank Edmonds' Crocodile, Punch, Judy and Joey.*

WEYMOUTH
& MR. PUNCH

All the World's a Stage

JUDITH STINTON

HARLEQUIN
PRESS

First published in England 2008 by
Harlequin Press
Allshire, East Anstey, Tiverton, EX16 9JG

Designed by Philip Lord

ISBN 97809 55922404

Printed by Biddles Ltd, King's Lynn, Norfolk, UK.

To Sheila and John Milton,
remembering the many happy times
we had together in Weymouth.

The boats, the sands, the esplanade,
The laughing crowd;
Light-hearted, loud
Greetings from some not ill-endowed.

The evening sunlit cliffs, the talk,
Hailings and halts,
The keen sea-salts,
The band, the Morgenblätter Waltz.

Thomas Hardy, 'At a Seaside Town in 1869'

Introduction

King George III changed the fortunes of Weymouth for ever when he chose to spend his summers in the town. The townsfolk were swift to respond to royal patronage, and the modest little spa soon acquired all the trappings, new or improved, of a much grander place. Assembly rooms, libraries, bathing machines, an esplanade and a theatre were provided for visitors, and the seafront was extended in the elegant curve still visible today.

Graced with a royal presence, the theatre eagerly laid on a variety of dramatic entertainments, ranging from Shakespeare to melodrama and harlequinade. Some of these entertainments had originated in Italy and France, and when they crossed over the Channel they developed their own distinctive English style.

Eventually, a number of the Weymouth 'theatricals' became associated mainly with the beach, which was increasingly becoming the centre of seaside holidays. These included the pierrot troupes, concert parties and Punch & Judy, all of which have deep and entangled roots. Of these, only Punch & Judy survived the Second World War, just as it had survived many other upheavals since its first known appearance on Weymouth sands around 1877.

Punch & Judy has an impressively long and enduring relationship with the resort. While tracing the history of the Weymouth shows, and those of the pierrots, this book is also an account – the first for over twenty years – of how Punch's show took shape through the centuries, and of how it came to the English seaside, and to Weymouth in particular. While following the story, some of the more unusual and charming features of the resort are explored, from the White Horse and the King's Statue – monuments to Weymouth's saviour – to the little spas and wells which ring the town. Without water, salt or spa, piped or tidal, there would have been no Weymouth.

The book is not a conventional history of the resort. Weymouth has already been well served by its local historian Maureen Attwooll, and by the thorough and sympathetic records of its buildings, drawn by the late Eric Ricketts. Rather, it is a selective account – a celebration – of a place which despite its architectural and geological importance, its role in Georgian history and that of the English seaside, and its part in the development of popular entertainment, has a tendency to be overlooked and underrated. This, as Mr. Punch might say, is a pity.

Many people have helped in the writing of this book. I'd especially like to thank Mark Poulton, Weymouth's current Punch & Judy professor, and his bottler Rene Smith. Other Punch & Judy professors who have contributed are Geoff Felix, Martin Bridle, John Styles, Wendy Wharam and the late Guy Higgins. Robert Leach kindly gave permission to quote from his works. As well as sweeping the chimney, John Stockley recalled Frank Edmonds' show and I spent an enjoyable morning looking at Edmonds' puppets in Roy Tomlinson's collection. In tracing the history of the Theatre Royal I was much helped by Georgina, Richard and Maxwell Grayson of Banus, by Stephen Mottram, David Brown, Colin Ellis, Professor Malcolm Airs, Jane Penoyre, John Wykes, Sally McGrath and the owners of Acutts. John Willows, curator of the Water Museum at Sutton Poyntz, provided much valuable information and encouragement. Maureen Attwooll too was extremely generous with her help.

Among the people in Weymouth who responded to my request for information were Sheila Milton, Margaret Morris, Joyce Otter, Charles Kind, Silvia Noakes, Pamela Haines, Pam Brady, Mr. B.King and Andrew Logan. Dawn Gould provided a lively account of childhood summers on the beach, and Joe Mullender was a tireless source of information. Other contributors were Peter Tolhurst, Clive Polden, Daphne Masterson, David and Tricia Grylls, Jean-Marc Pascal and Ray DaSilva. I am particularly grateful to Philip Lord for designing the book.

I'd also like to thank the staff of Weymouth Reference Library, Weymouth Museum, Portland Museum, the Dorset County Museum, the Dorset History Centre and the late-lamented Theatre Museum, Covent Garden. The Estate of John Cowper Powys gave their permission to quote from his works.

Finally, for the photographs, thanks go to Barry Cuff, 'Uncle Tacko', Rene Smith, Geoff Hounsell, Roy Tomlinson, Andy Hutchings, Wendy Wharam and Clive Polden. I would particularly like to thank Val Dicker of the Dorset County Museum for her assistance.

Cover 32, 57, Weymouth Reference Library. Frontispiece, Robert Leach. Title page 67, 71, 97, Roy Tomlinson Half title page, 75, Guy Higgins.1, 3, 22, 78, 82, Barry Cuff. 2, 30, 44, 48, 86, 87, the author. 4, 28, 29, 70, 73, Andy Hutchins. 5, 12, Portland Museum. 6, Mark Poulton. 10, Morine Krissdóttir. 13, 74, 77, 81, 98, Dorset County Museum. 23, 25, 26, 27, 'Uncle Tacko'. 24, 55, 76, Weymouth Museum. 33, 49, Stephen Mottram. 34, Richard Southern. 35, Richard Searle. 45, 79, Geoff Hounsell. 53, 54, Terry Hackman. 56, Mary Evans Picture Library. 80, 91, 92, Rene Smith. 84, 85, Dorset Echo. 90, Wendy Wharam. 93, Clive Polden. 95, 96, David Brown.

Contents

'Weymouth Sands'

Worked at Book about Weymouth. I am rather proud of my skill in gathering up the Various Puppets of this Planetary Book between Sea & Land – This book on the <u>Beach</u>.

Diary of John Cowper Powys, June 19 1933

Midnight shakes the memory
As a madman shakes a dead geranium.

T.S.Eliot, 'Rhapsody on a Windy Night'

WEYMOUTH WAS the most significant of all earthly places to the writer John Cowper Powys. Yet he wasn't born there – but at Shirley, Derbyshire, in 1872 – nor did he ever spend more than a few months at a time there. His paternal grandmother lived at Penn House, a Victorian addition to the Georgian Brunswick Terrace, and young

John enjoyed some very happy holidays on Weymouth sands. Later, his father Charles, vicar of Montacute in Somerset, retired to nearby Greenhill Terrace, to a house which, like his mother's, bordered the beach. Weymouth was, Powys wrote, 'of all places...the one most constantly familiar to me from my earliest infancy'. The great curve of the bay, the chalk cliffs, the stone island of Portland and the sixteen-mile stretch of Chesil Beach were like parts of his very being. In his *Autobiography* Powys described how 'every aspect of the Weymouth coast sunk into my mind with such a transubstantiating magic that it might be said that when I think now of certain things I think <u>with</u> St. John's spire and the Nothe, and the old Backwater, and the Harbour Bridge... Yes, it is through the medium of these things that I envisage all the experiences of my life; and so it will be to the end.'

John's memories of the seaside town extended back to a time before he had seen anything of Weymouth beyond the beach. In the *Autobiography* he recalls how his father would return to Shirley from

Weymouth with stirring stories of the place until 'all the well-known sea-marks there...were imprinted on my imagination'. Reality was even richer. So close was Penn House to the beach that life spilled over between house and sands. John wrote, 'To my childish senses there was a constant interpenetration between the whole seashore and the interior of this house; the spray and the foam and the jelly-fish and the starfish floating in and floating out all the while...'

2 Penn House, Brunswick Terrace, in a modern photograph.

The sands which he knew so well were divided in his mind between wet and dry, a distinction he often makes in his writing. In the opening pages of his first Wessex novel, *Wolf Solent* (1929), Wolf remembers his own early preference for 'the great shimmering expanse of wet sand, out beyond the bathing-machines, over the hot, dry sand under the sea-wall, where the donkeys stood and Punch and Judy was played.' The wet sands are the sands of childhood, like those in Robert Louis Stevenson's poem 'At the Seaside' from his *Child's Garden of Verses*, 1885:

> *When I was down beside the sea*
> *A wooden spade they gave to me*
> *To dig the sandy shore.*
> *My holes were empty like a cup,*
> *In every hole the sea came up,*
> *Till it could come no more.*

3 *Sand pictures, 1900s. Competitions and displays have been a regular feature on Weymouth beach.*

Fluid, ever-changing, glittering under the sun, in Powys's writings these sands are contrasted with the sands of adulthood which are arid and worn. Wet and dry are balanced; they can never be merged, neither can one overwhelm the other.

When John was seven, his father was appointed curate of St. Peter's, Dorchester – a demotion Charles Powys accepted so as to be nearer to his mother – and the family moved to Rothesay House in Dorchester's South Walks Road. Weymouth was now only a few miles away, and the Brunswick Terrace house must sometimes have been completely full, as John was the eldest of eleven children. Whenever they arrived there, he remembered, the cry would immediately go up 'Make tea!'. (They were a great family for tea-drinking.) The ceremony was presided over by their grandmother, widow of the Rector of Stalbridge in North Dorset, described by John in his autobiography as the children's 'aged relative'. (She is in fact fortunate to receive any description – other women get even shorter shrift. John's wife, mother and sisters are not mentioned at all in the autobiography.) For a slightly fuller portrait we must turn to John's brother Llewelyn, who recalled his grandmother as 'a fragile old lady of eighty...a delicate and brittle doll'.

The Misses Meade, aunts of the novelist John Meade Falkner, were near-neighbours of Mrs. Powys. They lived in number 5, at the town end of the row, which had originally been called Brunswick Buildings. Falkner dryly noted that more recent inhabitants, 'vulgar landladies', regarded the Georgian term 'Buildings' as lower-class, and the row became known (though not to Falkner, who persisted in using the old name) as Brunswick Terrace. 'The old Georgian dignity took wings and flew away.'

Brunswick Terrace is where Weymouth's arc of sand becomes covered in pebbles, and where the beach begins to shelve. (The pebbles shift inexorably towards the sands and repeated attempts have been made to halt their progress.) This was also where the water was deep enough for the fishermen to draw in their nets, and where a red post marked the point beyond which nude male bathing was allowed.

4 One of the 'fairy-story' goat carriages.

Llewelyn, whose affection for Weymouth almost matched John's own, wrote about a family holiday there in 1888, when he was four years old. He remembered the sea change at Penn House: 'In my child's mind the sea front was always separated into two strict divisions. To the right as I came out of the door was all the gaiety of a Vanity Fair, with varnished pleasure boats, entertainment shows, fairy-story goat-carriages, and white flat happy sands good for building castles.' During his adventures in this direction, Llewelyn takes cover in the midst of a crowd watching a Punch & Judy show, apparently (since he does not remark on it) already a regular part of the beach entertainments.

Turning out of the house to the left was a very different experience. There was 'a more sombre expanse where the sea was rough and had to be kept by banks of heavy pebbles from breaking over into Lodmoor, that wild waste of bird-haunted marshland. It was upon the top of these great beaches to the more serious east that real fishing boats were stabled, true deep-sea fishing-boats, hollow and benched.'

Recurring, and dangerous, tuberculosis made Llewelyn's memories of his childhood more acute. John's own memories were honed by his exile. His novel about the seaside town, *Weymouth Sands*, was written while he was living far away across the Atlantic and at a time when he

5 *Llewelyn Powys with Mr. Hill, last licensed bathchair man in Weymouth, 1930s.*

and his companion Phyllis Playter were becoming restless. Moves were being mentioned, and the couple did in fact settle in England in 1934. When John was beginning the book, Llewelyn sent him Weymouth guides and photographs to help jog his memory. These *aides-mémoire* brought their own difficulties at the start, as John felt that he was writing from the outside rather than from 'some inner *Entelecheia*' and that they slowed his progress. When he did find his way back into writing, despite his holiday memories the result was far from idyllic. In her book *John Cowper Powys and the Magical Quest*, Morine Krissdóttir has noted how 'superimposed on that world of glinting summer sunlight are the perceptions of a neurosis-blighted winter-ridden adult'. Like Llewelyn, John describes Weymouth's crowded summer beach – but his is a rather different one, when seen through the eyes of cynical young Peg Frampton. Peg notices 'the performers, the comic singers, the onlookers, the chaffing boys, the satyrish leers of the old men'. John's viewpoint can also be loftier than his brother's. Like a conjurer, he summons up Weymouth's circling landmarks: 'the spire of

St. John's church, the rounded stucco-façade of Number One Brunswick Terrace and of Number One St. Mary's Street, the Jubilee Clock, the Nothe, the Statue of George the Third' which 'seemed to emerge gigantically from a mass of vapourous unreality'. This litany of names recurs in varying patterns throughout the book, as if their incantation will bring the landmarks back to life for the exile.

A similar technique had been used – though to different effect – by Virginia Woolf in her novel *Mrs. Dalloway* (1925). Stepping out one June morning, the morning of her party, Clarissa Dalloway hears the solemn chimes of Big Ben. 'There! Out it boomed. First a warning, musical; then the hour, irrevocable. The leaden circles dissolved in the air.' The sound unites all who hear it. 'Heaven only knows why one loves it so…but the veriest frumps, the most dejected of miseries sitting on doorsteps (drink their downfall) do the same...' This is what Clarissa loves: 'life; London; this moment of June.' Within this precise geography, that indefinable thing, memory, is stirred in the characters, as it is in *Weymouth Sands*. But there are differences in the way the two places affect those who live in them. Virginia Woolf's London is an intimate, coherent place, where most of the characters are comfortable in their surroundings. Few people in *Weymouth Sands* achieve this ease, this reciprocality. Perdita Wane tells her lover, Jobber Skald: 'I heard Mr. Muir talking to Mr. Cobbold the other night about the shape of Portland as he sees it from his window. It's quaint to think of <u>his</u> landscape being your home and <u>your</u> landscape being his home.' The landscape is more than just Jobber's home. The cerebral observer Muir resists integration; Jobber, stonemason's son, belongs to the land – though even he is subservient to it. For Powys the Weymouth landmarks 'in their long confederacy' have become like an 'organic Being', a vast and powerful abstraction dominating and controlling the inhabitants.

In both *Mrs. Dalloway* and *Weymouth Sands*, unity is brought to all manner of people by the forces of a single place, and so, for both Woolf and Powys, real place names with all their resonances are vital to their effects. Originally, though, as the result of a libel case

Powys had to make considerable changes to the English version of *Weymouth Sands.*

In 1934, after the publication in England of his second Wessex novel *A Glastonbury Romance*, Powys and his English publisher John Lane were sued by the owner of the Wookey Hole caves near Wells, Somerset. The caves featured in the novel under the proprietorship of Philip Crow. The real owner, Wing Commander Gerald Hodgkinson, claimed that he was the model for Crow, and that John's description of the caves would deter visitors. The case was eventually settled out of court, but in the meantime John Lane nervously delayed the publication of *Weymouth Sands.* In previous novels, Powys had followed Thomas Hardy in disguising the names of places, but now, at a moment when the real names actually counted, he was obliged to change them. *Weymouth Sands* was first published in England as *Jobber Skald*, the name of a major (though not the most important) character. Even worse, Weymouth becomes 'an English coastal town' and Lodmoor 'a peat bog'. The Jubilee Clock becomes 'the Council Clock' – not much cause for celebration here. It was as if in *Mrs. Dalloway*, Virginia Woolf had been obliged to call Big Ben 'the Official Timekeeper'. Probably because of these enforced changes, the litanies of names were omitted, much to the detriment of the book. Not until 1963 did the novel appear in England as *Weymouth Sands*, with the true place names restored and repeated.

Unchanged, though, from *Jobber Skald* to *Weymouth Sands* is the seaside Punch & Judy show. One performance begins the novel, another provides a set-piece near the book's end. In between, the show's characters, structure and imagery are used in the shaping of the work.

The book opens on Weymouth beach on a dank dark January afternoon (the novel takes place over the course of a year) where a 'belated' Punch & Judy show is being performed under the cold stone walls of the Esplanade by the Jubilee Clock. A scanty group of bystanders are watching 'an especially violent' Punch. The puppeteer's daughters, Marret and Tiny Jones, are his bottlers, collecting

6 Punch & Judy man, James Murray, performing by the Jubilee Clock.

the money in bags which dangle from discouragingly 'forlorn poles'. Jones himself is glimpsed just briefly, and for the only time in the novel. He is 'a pallid and spasmodic individual with a face like a hungry rat'. Later Powys casually lets slip that Jones, like his chief puppet, has beaten his children's mother to death. Jones has done it with a jug full of water – and she was a woman who hated getting wet. There may be another joke here too. 'Mr. Jones', master of Toby, was sometimes a character in Punch & Judy, arguing with Punch over the dog's true ownership.

This dismal performance is observed by Magnus Muir, 'tutor in Latin to backward boys'. The antics of the 'especially violent' and deranged Punch act as a prologue to the appearance of the neurotic Sylvanus Cobbald. Cobbald, an itinerant preacher, gives a rival performance on the Esplanade, pouring forth incomprehensible 'spiritual revelations' while the beach show reaches its grisly climax. These two men, Muir and Cobbald, were – Powys freely admitted – taken from himself. They seemed, he noted in his essay *Remembrances*, 'the left and right rib so to speak of my own skeleton'. Like Mr. Punch – and John Cowper Powys – Magnus carries a stick. The stick, which belonged to his late father, 'protruded upwards from his side as he walked, making an acute angle from his body' when he puts his cold hands into his pockets. Unlike Mr. Punch, mild Magnus does not use it to hit anyone, but the stick has become a part of his character, his stage business, its movements described at Magnus's every entrance.

Powys's other half, Sylvanus the preacher, is a charismatic and moustachioed figure with a devoted female following – despite his curious appearance. He is able to 'hold his neck extended' at will, like a tortoise. This trick does not surprise Marret the Punch & Judy girl, who, accustomed to her father's grotesque puppets, assumes that such movements are 'the natural emotional expression of the human frame'. Such actions, however, might be thought to belong rather within the puppet frame, recalling those of the mysterious being who strays mutely into John Payne Collier's fanciful version of Punch & Judy (1828), the first and most influential published script of the play. This 'Nobody' is given eerie shape by George Cruikshank's accompanying illustration:

> Enter a figure dressed like a courtier, who sings a slow air, and moves to it with great gravity and solemnity. He first takes off his hat on the right of the theatre, and then on the left, and carries it in his hand. He then stops in the centre; the music ceases, and suddenly his throat begins to elongate, and his head gradually rises until his neck is taller than all the rest of his body. After pausing for some time, the head sinks again, and, as soon as it has descended to its natural place, the figure exits.

Sylvanus possesses a similarly eerie, transient quality and eventually he reminds even the besotted Marret of one of Mr. Jones's puppets, after she sees him speaking 'with a sardonic grimace that made his long white face wrinkle up like the Ghost in her father's repertoire'. Sylvanus, it seems, has only a flimsy grasp of this mortal world.

More frequently, however, rather than recalling puppets of the Punch & Judy show, characters resemble figures from the Italian Commedia dell'Arte, from which Punch himself is mainly derived. The Commedia dell'Arte (which roughly translates as 'Comedy of the Artists') flourished in Italy during the sixteenth and seventeenth centuries, performed by wandering troupes of actors. Their plays were improvised from a set of scenarios, dependent on actor rather than on

7 'A figure dressed like a courtier', otherwise known as 'Nobody'.
Drawing by George Cruikshank.

dramatist's script, giving the performers the freedom to amuse the
audience with their *lazzi*: their comedy and acrobatics. Wearing his
character's mask, an actor would play one part throughout his life,
losing his own identity in the process or merging it with the role
he played, and creating a separate persona. Many of the stock
characters – the 'Masks' – in the Commedia plays can also be found
in *Weymouth Sands*, characters such as Harlequin, the Doctor,
Pantaloon and Pierrot.

Sylvanus's brother Jerry, for instance, is a famous professional
clown, the greatest clown in the English theatre. He has 'the eye of a
philosophical harlequin', and dresses in a gaudy motley 'of his own
making'. He has bought the 'old-fashioned' Regents Theatre where he
performs to audiences who have not been so splendidly entertained
since the days of George III. (An actual Regent Theatre and Dance Hall
opened in Weymouth in 1929, around the time in which the novel
is set.) Jerry lives above and beyond the town in the stone-fronted

8 Arlecchino or Harlequin.

High House, Greenhill, in uncomfortable rooms furnished with tarnished gold. He has a mobile face which he can reinvent 'at any moment'. This man of many masks, this chameleon, is loved by women. Like his Italian equivalent, the ever-changing *Arlecchino*, Jerry is a subtle, shifting, treacherous character. Only in the company of Dr. Lucky Girodel, 'notorious quack, empiric, and abortion-procurer' does Jerry reveal his true face.

Lucky himself, like *Il Dottore*, the Doctor (usually a doctor of law) in the Commedia dell'Arte, is a loquacious man – 'chattering *sans cesse*' – and restless with it, mincing round the room with a 'sort of lively formality' in his tight striped trousers. In both the English and Italian variants of this role the Doctor is partial to drink, and Lucky follows in that tradition. We are told that even his wallpaper is the brackish colour of Cattistock & Frampton's cheapest Weymouth ales.

Lucky is one of the three doctors, all of them charlatans, in *Weymouth Sands*. Not one is a credit to his calling. Of the other two, Dr. Higginbottom is the ineffectual locum, and Dr. Daniel Brush, more bizarrely, is a vivisector (to Powys the most evil of creatures). Dr. Brush operates somewhat off-stage on the Dorset downs, in a 'Hell's Museum' which doubles as a lunatic asylum. This devilish figure is barely sketched, almost as if his creator could not quite bring himself to describe him. Disappointingly faceless, Brush is still awaiting a mask.

Dr. Brush's brother-in-law, 'Dog' Cattistock, is a wealthy brewer. His financial activities threaten the livelihood of the Portland stone-masons when he declares his intention of closing the largest quarry on the island, and he has already earned the enmity of Jobber Skald after cheating the latter's quarryman father. Cattistock is only about forty years old, yet his hair has grown 'prematurely thin and grey' and his 'forward-jutting' chin permanently bristles with 'sharp thick light-coloured hair'. Although young for the role, he comes on as *Pantalone*, a powerful man with a jerky strutting walk 'as if consciously pushing his way through serried ranks of antagonists'. He is rich yet miserly, living in fear that his intended bride will squander all of his cherished wealth, a fear which keeps him awake at night.

Figures such as these, deriving from the Commedia plays, are not naturalistic, they are rarely altered by events; the masks are returned unchanged to their box at the end of the performance. Like many a character from John Cowper Powys's novels they are defined by a single trait. Powys is employing stock characters, but at the same time he is making them his own, just as the Commedia actors used to do.

Such an approach does not necessarily make his characters totally uncomplicated. Jerry Cobbald is as various as his garb and, for better or worse, Lucky remains enigmatically elusive. Meanwhile, too, the major characters stand apart from this street theatre, being generally more complex and more human. Magnus Muir, for example, is still living in the shadow of his dead father and this inhibits him romantically. (As he himself acknowledges,

9 *Pantalone or Pantaloon.*

'There's something contemptible about the love affairs of a timid person.') However, he remains respected as a teacher and has courage enough to confront an angry parent when the occasion requires it.

The female characters in *Weymouth Sands* are more wooden: the young girls are like a set of knowing dolls. They have tiny, diminutive names, such as Curly, Tissty, Tossty and Peg. Two older women, Jerry Cobbald's wife Lucinda and her sister Hortensia Lily, are more elaborately carved, being compared to the figure-heads of ships. (They are indeed the daughters of a sea captain.) The seductive Mrs. Lily reminds Jobber Skald of the head adorning 'a ramshackle craft, long since gone to the bottom…her figure-head had always stuck in his memory; and her queer name too. She was called the Medusa.' Jerry Cobbald is engaged in a perpetual struggle to keep the rigid mask of his statuesque wife in place.

Lonely Perdita Wane seems to be the only female character taken seriously by the author, and only Perdita – the lost girl from *A Winter's Tale* – and her lover Jobber Skald achieve any real sexual fulfilment. For this is the literature of frustration. Of the two characters deriving from Powys himself, Magnus Muir is (unsurprisingly) a cuckold and Sylvanus Cobbald a sort of religious vampire, believing that 'only in the souls of women' will he find immortality. This obsession, which mirrors Magnus's own hopeless courtship of the young Curly Wix, brings about Sylvanus's downfall. He is incarcerated in the ghastly Hell's Museum.

Watching the Punch & Judy show among the high season crowds, Magnus observes that 'Punch must be the eternal embodiment of…the essential masculine element in every living man'. Supremely misogynistic, Punch is trapped in a world of violence, from which he can escape only by instigating further attacks. While the violence in *Weymouth Sands* is always imminent rather than actual the threat of it is ever present, in a welter of futile phallic symbols – sticks, stones, posts and canes.

The action of the novel takes place through a series of scenes in which a character will make a brief appearance and then disappear, usually reappearing several chapters later, rather as puppets do in a Punch & Judy show. This picaresque structure works well enough within the confines of a short show, but is less satisfactory when employed in a full-length book, one where too many characters are in any case left dangling. Very little actually happens – in fact the story is conspicuous for two events which never take place – the wedding of Dog Cattistock and Hortensia Lily, and the taking of revenge by Jobber on his enemy the would-be bridegroom.

In *John Cowper Powys and the Magical Quest*, Morine Krissdóttir finds the structure of *Weymouth Sands* 'slack and disoriented…the numerous sub-plots are not held together as they usually are by the tension of the author, but allowed to fly off and float into extinction like sparks from an untended fire'. One explanation for this could be that 'in some curious way, setting the novel in the town of Weymouth was disruptive'. Powys himself was aware of the problem. He thought his new novel gentler than his earlier ones – more like a water-colour than an oil-painting – and also lighter and more humorous. He conceded in a letter to his brother Llewelyn (May 7 1933) that the plot was 'weak and not very convincing'. But, he concluded, why should such an 'exciting' book as *Weymouth Sands* 'not be able to dispense with the teasing necessity of a Plot?' The novel should stand or fall by its characters. (This also holds true for a Commedia performance, where plot can be a mere formality.)

It is the descriptions of Weymouth which bind the book together: fluid, evocative and haunting, they are the most memorable descriptions ever written of the much-fêted seaside town. Powys's avowed concern in the book is 'to show how there is something in human life that by slow degrees creates a reciprocity between itself and any particular scene where it has existed, and lived and moved and been happy and sad, for a considerable number of years.' To explore this process he is relying on his own memories, made more poignant by the double distancing of time and ocean, and shaped by more conventional maps and guides. Apart from the Hell's Museum – as vaguely located as its namesake – streets and building are easily identifiable.

His Weymouth is also seen through the eyes of his father Charles, just as Magnus Muir sees it through his own father's eyes in the novel. (It is telling that Powys completed *Weymouth Sands* in July 1933 and in the next month, on the Feast of the Assumption, he began to write his *Autobiography*, of which the earlier chapters were much concerned with this parent.) His father was on his mind. John had seen Weymouth in his imagination through his father's stories before he had seen much of the real place, and these pictures must have sometimes remained more vivid to him than the actuality. Again as for his alter-ego Magnus Muir, for John Cowper Powys each landmark was a 'sacred hieroglyph': a piece of his father's life.

> How well he knew this spot! It was one of those geographical points on the surface of the planet that would surely rush into his mind when he came to die, as a concentrated essence of all that life meant! It was on this bench that he had sat five years ago when his father died.

Other characters make their own responses to the town. The mad boy Larry Zed experiences Weymouth on an almost subterranean level: that of the 'great cold-bodied eels' in the wet mud of Lodmoor and of the 'vapour ghosts' of the mist that he sees as he crashes his way across the shingle. The 'sluggish and unambitious' Rodney Loder, who works for his lawyer father, relies for escape from his humdrum life on reveries about his Weymouth walks, reliving them over and over again 'until they acquired for him a sort of mystical value, as if they were the casual by-paths or hidden postern-gates, leading into aerial landscapes of other and much happier incarnations'. Rodney is something of a lost soul, a shadowy, latterday Pierrot, yet another of the characters deriving ultimately from the Commedia dell'Arte plays. He has a 'grave full face' with a close-fitting cap of chestnut hair and a 'clear white parting'. Born '*triste*', he nurses a longing for a 'certain little painted dwelling' he once glimpsed near the Seine at St. Cloud in Paris – Paris, which was the city where Pierrot experienced his subtlest incarnation.

John Cowper Powys himself was yet another sort of Pierrot. His larger-than-life, somewhat stagy personality lent itself to role-playing. In the house that he shared with Phyllis Playter in upstate New York, Powys worked on *Weymouth Sands*, and played teasing games with his lover. In the games he was Petrushka (a Russian derivative of Pierrot) and she was his Dancer: two figures from Stravinsky's ballet of 1911, *Petrushka*. The ballet is set in St. Petersburg some time in the 1830s, when a Shrove Tuesday Fair is taking place. A puppet show, akin to a Punch & Judy performance, provides one of the entertainments. Three puppets are brought to life by the Showman: Petrushka, his rival the Moor and the Dancer. Like most Pierrots, Petrushka is unlucky in love, and he is rejected by the Dancer. The Moor kills the jealous Petrushka, but he reappears as a ghost at the end of the show. This *jeu d'esprit* features frequently in Powys's diaries of the time, and Phyllis did in fact attend a performance of the ballet in London in 1935. There may also have been yet another dimension to Powys's and Playter's game.

10 *John Cowper Powys and Phyllis Playter as 'Petrushka and the Dancer'.*

The Pierrot of the period was one allied to the moon and thence to sterility. The couple had no children, except for two imaginary ones – Tony and Perdita Stone.

Just as a character in Punch & Judy like Mr. Jones can become a puppeteer, so the author, the archetypal puppeteer, can become a puppet. As powerless and manipulated as any puppets, the characters in *Weymouth Sands* move helplessly against a backcloth of sea and sky and resounding landmarks. From his exile, remembering, Powys summons up what for him was the spirit of the place.

> Was there any town in the world by the English sea that equalled this old Georgian resort? It was so integral with itself, and it seemed now, in that August haze, as if it had risen in its complete totality – Spire and Statue and Nothe and Backwater and all its ivory-misted rows of houses – straight out of the glittering bay. It seemed an immaterial, an insubstantial thing to him just then, a thing made of the stuff of thought! It was as if in all its long nights and days an impalpable thought-image of it had been wrought, that on such an afternoon as this substituted itself for the solid reality.

Like a dream palace, Weymouth is surrounded by water, lake and marsh as well as sea. Radipole Lake was once the town's tidal Backwater, as Peg Frampton recalls in *Weymouth Sands*:

> The girl was old enough to remember the time, before the building of the new Westham Bridge, when Swan Villa had overlooked the tidal Backwater. Some of her happiest childish memories were connected with these muddy, brackish reaches, on the edge of which she used to play for hours, imbibing the sour tidal smells and watching the swans and the wild ducks. But the Backwater had been transformed into an

ornamental basin, rendered independent of the sea-tides; and although its smooth expanse of harmless water, like a pond in a Public Park, still stretched away as far as Radipole Village, a couple of miles from the old Harbour Bridge, the charm of the salt mud-pools and the tidal débris remained in her mind as something she missed.

On the seaward side of the town lies Lodmoor marsh. Since the publication of *Weymouth Sands* it too has been diminished by development. It was very different then, as long-time resident Sheila Milton remembers from her childhood.

> In those far-off days, Lodmoor marsh really was wild and deserted, apart from the gulls forever sweeping over in crowds, calling, and there were hawks and other birds. The hills to the east which surrounded the marsh were green with few, if any, buildings to be seen. It seemed an exciting and slightly scary place, especially when the clouds came and the wind blew.

Lodmoor would often flood, especially in a rainy winter, when heavy seas would leach through the shingle of the storm beach and under the sea wall. At such times, the sea could reach as far inland as two Mile Copse, and the water would lie there for weeks. The drainage channels which ran down to the sluice gardens (now an enclave of chalets and paddling pools) failed to prevent the floods.

Along the road which divides Lodmoor from its sea was a turnpike cottage, a half-way house described in *Weymouth Sands* as a 'melancholy little erection, with its white-washed walls and its black-tarred roof, over-topped by tall bill-boards bearing weather-stained advertisements.' The house had its own small garden containing vegetation and a brown and white cow called Blotchy – suddenly, we are in earthier territory.

In the toll house lives Gipsy May, follower and admirer of Sylvanus Cobbald, and the idiot boy Larry Zed, who was formerly a patient in the Hell's Museum. They are visited by Gipsy May's rival in love, Marret

Jones, who has been lured to Lodmoor to have her fortune told. (Such a fortune-teller, Anita Gypsy Lee, palmist and clairvoyant, can still be seen on the Esplanade in Weymouth during the summer season.) In the novel, mystic May uses ordinary playing cards as well as her Tarot pack of 'Egyptian cards'. The last card to come face up is the ominous *Hanged Man*. Marret, afraid that this card applies to Sylvanus, and that the gallows will be his fate, consoles herself by declaring that 'there be other gallowses in the world, beyon' they silly pictures'. Gipsy May will have none of this.

> 'Twas..the..Hanged..Man..that..were..thik..last card,' she gasped out, in a low, solemn voice, as if the mere mention of this formidable symbol were a sacrilege. 'And you knowed it were! Didn't you hear her say, Larry, that there were other gallowses than what be in my cards? She were talking of thik wold Punch, and of his being hanged for Judy. Hanged for Judy! – when all the time it were the *Hanged Man* of me girt Egyptian cards what fell down…'Tweren't no mommet in no doll's-house theayter what fell down…'twas the…Hanged…Man.'

Either woman could have been right in her interpretation. In his classic commentary on the Tarot, originally published in 1910 and much reprinted, A.E.Waite observes that the Hanged Man has 'great significance, but all the significance is veiled'. He suggests that 'it expresses the relation, in one of its aspects, between the Divine and the Universe'. In *Weymouth Sands*, Sylvanus is a somewhat shaky bridge between God and the World. He does escape the gallows, only to end in the clutches of the Devil – in the shape of Dr. Brush.

Another gallows, Weymouth's place of execution in the Monmouth Rebellion, was conveniently nearby, in the area of modern Greenhill Gardens. Here twelve men were executed by order of the deranged Judge Jeffreys in 1685 to teach the inhabitants a lesson: sixteen quarters and six heads were displayed around Weymouth. This

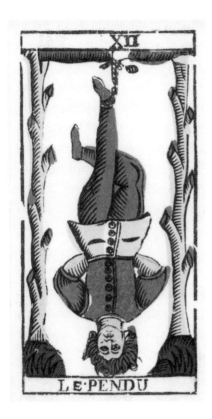

11 The Hanged Man Tarot card.

was despite the fact that the town had not been implicated in the disastrous uprising led by the Duke of Monmouth, illegitimate son of Charles II, against his half-brother, James II. (The only local person involved was an unfortunate young barber's apprentice who had publicly read out Monmouth's proclamation and was sentenced to be whipped at every market town in the county each year for seven years.) Of other hangings, few are recorded. A solitary pirate met his end there, and two people were executed during the English Civil War. These were the exceptions. In 1571, the current Mayor had been granted the right to hold Sessions of the Peace in the town. These Quarter Sessions did not usually try capital cases which would be sent to the Assizes at Dorchester, and there any executions would be carried out.

Both geography and history left Lodmoor a place away from the town. Its name is thought by some to derive from the Saxon *Lodomor*, meaning a moor not held in common, but divided into lots, with several holders. However, there would have been little point in dividing a bog into segments, and the name is more likely to have come from the Celtic *lutä*, meaning 'mud'. Unlike Chesil Beach on the other side of Weymouth, Lodmoor is low-lying, both flooded by the sea and `draining back into it under the shingle. Part salt-marsh, part grass and rushes, it was home to eels and otters, and the scene of some quiet poaching. In his essay on Lodmoor, Llewelyn Powys wrote of how 'in the old days when the poor of Weymouth were allowed free access to these marshlands, jersey-wearing sportsmen were content to wait for hours in the bitterest winds on the chance of supplying a cottage kitchen down by the harbour with a plump widgeon'. There was, too, a fair amount of smuggling, as there was almost everywhere along the Dorset coast. Though controls were tight around Weymouth Harbour, places like Lulworth and Fleet were notorious smuggling centres. In the mid-nineteenth century, the local smugglers came from the Black House, a derelict old public house just beyond Greenhill. The smugglers were a family named Knight. As John Meade Falkner remembered from his childhood they were 'tall, lank men', dark, solemn and separate. By day they worked as wheel-chairmen, 'taciturn and well-behaved'. The night was their own and they used it to their advantage. Like many a smugglers' base, the Black House was said to have its own secret passage – a sluice-pipe leading into the marshes. When the old inn was destroyed by fire, it was not rebuilt and so a source of trouble was conveniently removed.

As both Falkner and Llewelyn Powys suggest in their memoirs, Lodmoor in the nineteenth century seemed to belong to the people. Falkner also remembered how 'In the strong heats of summer a shimmering haze often wrapped the flats in mystery, and in the winter it was the first place to freeze. Then all younger Weymouth went out to skate, there were barrows of buns and apples and ginger-beer…' Since the town has a temperate, sunny climate, the youth of Weymouth made the most of any rare opportunity to take to the ice.

For a while from 1821 to the 1890s, part of Lodmoor was used as a race course, unlikely as this may sound. The races took place at the end of every August at Overcombe Corner – more Bowleaze Cove than Weymouth – and lasted for three days. In Thomas Hardy's *Far From the Madding Crowd*, set in the mid-nineteenth century, Sergeant Troy, a racing man, complains about the meeting, which he describes as being at the edge of 'Budmouth' (Hardy's usual name for Weymouth) on a gusty autumn day.

'Never did I see such a day as 'twas! 'Tis a wild open place, just out of Budmouth, and a drab sea rolled in towards us like liquid misery. Wind and rain – good Lord! Dark? Why 'twas as black as my hat before the last race was run. 'Twas five o'clock, and you couldn't see the horses till they were almost in, let alone colours. The ground was as heavy as lead, and all judgement from a fellow's experience went for nothing. Horses, riders, people, were all blown about like ships at sea.'

Even in the 1930s it was easy to get lost on Lodmoor. Sheila Milton remembers that 'there was said to be a safe path from the farmlands to the sea; we could not find it. You always came up to a deep dyke or very marshy patch.' Her aim was to reach the toll house, by then redundant (at the time when John Cowper Powys was writing *Weymouth Sands*) and occupied by a carter named Sugar'em Shorey. Generations of Shoreys had occupied the little house, and Sugar'em was said to have got his name from an expression his grandfather Albert used. Whenever he outwitted someone in a business deal Albert would declare, with great satisfaction, 'We sugared 'em!'

12 *Sugar'em Shorey's tollhouse cottage* c.1928.

'Everyone was quite scared of him. So I don't know what we would have done had he charged out of his hut and shouted at us and waved his whip. He wandered around the town in winter selling paraffin and wood from an old cart, drawn by a rather sad pony. In summer he could be seen driving a large open carriage with seats to Upwey Wishing Well.' The cottage, where he lived with his sister, was 'old and dilapidated and covered with tarred tiles and tarpaulin. It appeared to be half buried in the turf, and was about half way along the sea-road to Overcombe, set back from the road.' This is much as it appears in *Weymouth Sands.*

The cottage disappeared overnight, bulldozed by Council employees in 1959. Sugar'em and his sister moved reluctantly to a prefab in Littlemoor Crescent; he was by then seventy-three years old. What remains of Lodmoor is now a nature reserve, and the Old Toll House Hide stands in place of the cottage. Llewelyn Powys had, presciently, written to the *Dorset Echo* in July 1933 suggesting that Weymouth Town Council should acquire the marsh for use as a bird sanctuary. As he reported in a letter to G.Bryer Ash, dated July 27 1933, 'I pointed out that Weymouth retained its distinction over other West Country watering places largely from the fact of having this tract of wild moorlands on one side of it and the romantic harbour on the other.' The Council could have bought a large area of Lodmoor cheaply when it was being sold by the Weld estate in 1925, but it was bought instead by a speculative builder, who had to abandon his ambitious schemes because of drainage problems. Llewelyn wanted to start a campaign for the public purchase of Lodmoor. 'If Lodmoor were once possessed in this way the poetic quality of Weymouth would be protected forever – no amount of cheap building could really standardize the town if it had this large acreage of reeds and rushes and shining dykes on its eastern side.'

Unhappily, his plea was disregarded. Lodmoor had a reprieve during the Second World War when the military authorities gave orders for the sluices to be opened and the marsh flooded once more. After the War, it once again became a prey to development with proposals for marinas, hotels and a mass of housing. It was even suggested as a suitable site for a rubbish dump. Development has been mainly by stealth, and now only a small area of marsh remains. Now it could stand as a monument to English municipal tidiness at its most obsessive. Like Radipole Lake, the rump of Lodmoor is well maintained by the Royal Society for the Protection of Birds, and is still alive with birds, some of them rare. But the spirit of Lodmoor, the wild otherness, has gone forever.

13 Eclipse of the sun on Lodmoor, June 29 1927 by the Revd Victor Tanner.

Pierrot

Au clair de la lune
Mon ami Pierrot
Prêtes-moi ta plume,
Pour écrire un mot.
Ma chandelle est morte.
Je n'ai plus de feu,
Ouvre-moi ta porte
Pour l'amour de Dieu.

Pierrot's song

O F ALL THE MANY Commedia dell'Arte characters, two are a part of the history of Punch & Judy. One, of course, is Pulcinella; the other one is Pierrot.

In *Weymouth Sands*, Rodney Loder – the palest of pale Pierrots – longs to be in Paris, which he sees as his spiritual home. Paris is the perfect setting for such a dream. It was the city where, in the mid-nineteenth century, Pierrot reached the zenith of his career. It had been a long and arduous journey for the character, and one which afterwards continued triumphantly out of France and into England – where he finally settled at the seaside.

Pierrot's story is one of increasing isolation. He began as a member of the European family of travelling comedians who came together in the sixteenth century and who took shape as the Commedia dell'Arte. They could be found in the fairs and carnivals of the Italian market places, where their role was a very simple one. In such crowded public areas, the (typically Venetian) mountebanks, quack doctors and pedlars would hawk their wares, magicians would flaunt their sleight of hand, and beggars hustled on every corner. Potential customers would be drawn in by figures wearing outlandish costumes and gargoyle-like masks who would not perform until the end of the business, after the money had been securely taken. Main characters were usually *Pantalone*, (Pantaloon), *Arlecchino* (Harlequin), *Pulcinella*, (Punch), the Captain, the Doctor, *Brighella* – meaning 'fool' or 'silly ass' – and *Pedrolino*, who in France was to become Pierrot.

Like the names of the other major Commedia characters, Pedrolino's would be altered from time to time and from place to place – though his perhaps changed more than anyone's. In Italy he was also called *Piero*, then *Pagliaccio* (from *pagliaio*, a pile of straw) and *Gian-Farina* (or *Jean Farin* when he moved to France). This last name came about because Pierrot, unlike other male stock characters, never wore a mask. His face was whitened with *farina* (flour), allowing him to use a wide range of facial expressions which the other characters – the Masks – were denied. His most famous and first interpreter as Pedrolino was Pedrolino Pellesini whose career lasted from about 1576 to 1614.

14 Mountebank with Pulcinella, Pedrolino and Harlequin.

The Commedia companies usually performed in family groups, and Pedrolino was traditionally played by the youngest son, who was at the bottom of the heap. He was expected to sleep amongst the animals and to care for them. In the plays, he was often in love with *Columbina* (Columbine), the servant girl who was the leading female figure, but would usually lose her to his fellow-servant, the more extravert Arlecchino. Pedrolino, Arlecchino, Brighella, and sometimes Pulcinella, were all *zanni*, or clowns.

Zanni – the Venetian diminutive of *Giovanni* – is a word that remains the same in both singular and plural. It could be used as the name of one Mask when the character was not further defined – or applied generally to all the *zanni*. A *zanni* had a voice like a market porter, both loud and harsh. The term does not translate exactly, but the nearest English equivalent word is 'zany'.

Pedrolino had a hard life. As he was accustomed to dodging blows, he was obliged to become increasingly agile: an acrobat. His hand-me-down clothes were usually too large, making him look like a scarecrow.

Perhaps because of the harsh treatment he received, and because he never wore a mask, he seemed at times more human, more sympathetic than other Commedia characters. He had a protean quality, his character reshaping at different times and in different places.

For practical reasons, the Commedia performers often used mime as they ventured through Italy, through France and through Spain – and as far afield as Russia, Czechoslovakia and Denmark. When they did speak they used Italian dialects, latterly Tuscan, Paduan and Venetian. According to John Rudlin in his book on the Commedia, Harlequin usually spoke with a 'guttural Bergamese dialect, hoarse from street hawking', while the lovers spoke Tuscan, the literary dialect of Italy. Local characters would take precedence in their home district, assuming an importance they might not have elsewhere. Masks continued to be used until the eighteenth century – though they were not the classical masks of grinning comedy or tearful tragedy, they were expressionless, making interpretation of the role much more demanding for the actor. Not being allowed to speak, too, or speaking only in a foreign tongue, gave the performer a muted eloquence.

Pagliaccio, 1600,
by Maurice Sand

Peppe-Nappa, 1770,
by Maurice Sand

Pedrolino, 1673,
by Maurice Sand

Though companies performed in France from the mid-sixteenth century, the Commedia dell'Arte did not became wholly established there until 1680, under the patronage of Charles IX's mother, the Italian Caterina de' Medici, when the players were appointed *Comédians Italiens du Roi* and had their own theatre in Paris at the Hôtel de Bourgogne. On their first arrival they performed in Italian: a language understood by most of the

15 *Early versions of Pierrot: Pagliaccio, Peppe-Nappa and Pedrolino.*

court. Later, they spoke in French and the significant year for Pedrolino was 1665 when he (or a figure very like him) began to change his name as well as his language. He appeared in Molière's play *Don Juan ou Le Festin de Pierre* as a peasant called Pierrot, and this was to become his most common name in France. Pierrot is of course a diminutive of Pierre, and was already used in French for a peasant or shepherd. Around the same time, an Italian actor called Giuseppe Giaratone (or Geratoni) joined the players and transformed Pedrolino into a Pierrot who showed signs of a greater sensitivity than earlier versions of the character had shown.

On occasion the actors lost their royal patronage, as they did for nineteen years from 1697 during the long reign of Louis XIV. It is said that the Sun King took serious offence at one of their plays, Molière's *La Fausse Prude,* because of its satirical references to his morganatic and unpopular wife, Madame de Maintenon. So the players had to resort to the fair of Saint-Germain des Près, which was the largest in Paris and (like Petrushka's) held on Shrove Tuesday, and to the autumn fair of Saint-Laurent. The fairs were an important feature of theatrical life in Paris, and their importance grew at the end of the seventeenth century when the booths were replaced by permanent playhouses, allowing for longer theatrical seasons.

Back in the fairground, Harlequin was initially the dominant character, while Pierrot revived his earlier skills as a tight-rope walker and acrobat. Though the characters were all forbidden to speak (asides were written on rolls of paper or a blackboard), they were permitted to sing, and Pierrot could still use his recently acquired skill as a ballad singer. Jean-Baptiste Hamoche, greatest fairground interpreter of Pierrot, performed *Au Clair de la Lune,* the song which became Pierrot's own at Hamoche's debut in 1712. Although the ballad has the apparent simplicity of a folk song, its origins were more sophisticated. The wistful music was composed by the French court composer, Jean-Baptiste Lully, to verses by his librettist, Philippe Quinault. In the song, Pierrot is associated with the moon and a candle.

17 Gilles.

Pierrot was changing again. In the fairgrounds he was often confused with Gilles, a simple provincial soul. Pierrot looks very like Gilles in Watteau's painting of 1721, produced as a billboard for the Théâtre de la Foire in Paris. In the portrait he comes over as a silken fop, straw-hatted still, yet with an elaborate frilled collar, symbols of his rustic origins and of his servitude. Nevertheless (as Richard Holmes has pointed out in a poignant essay from his collection *Sidetracks*) in the midst of his trappings his real, raw face has emerged at last, stripped of its floury disguise.

In Italy during the same period, Pierrot was known as Peppe-Nappa, dressed in a costume hung with pompoms and with long, flapping sleeves, a forerunner of the feeble phantom he was to become so much later in England. These pompoms were dignified by a legend, in which they were shown to be the mark of a Pierrot. The story went that a small, naked boy was found by St. Peter wandering outside the gates of Heaven. It was winter, and when St. Peter picked the child up, the snow on his body was transformed into clothing. The saint took the foundling in, naming him Pierrot (or 'little Peter'). Heedless of the saint's command, the boy wandered out of Paradise to play once more with mortal children. When he returned, his white garments were dotted with black fingerprints. Pierrot had disobeyed St. Peter and was expelled from Heaven, his pompoms a token of his disobedience.

By the end of the century Commedia dell'Arte had ceased to exist in Italy. The Italian playwright Carlo Goldoni, ironically the first person to use the term 'Commedia dell'Arte', was writing fully-scripted plays in the genre, with no room for improvisation, and was also insisting that the characters remove their masks. The end result was a different genre. In France the patrons had gone too, swept away by the Revolution. Unlike Louis XVI, though, Pierrot survived – in his own way – by changing his shape once again. He was no longer a country-man, he became a dedicated city dweller, discarding his rustic hat in the process.

It was at this transitional stage in his life that Pierrot – so the story goes – encountered Napoleon Bonaparte. The Emperor saw Pierrot's limp and hopeless figure lying in the road as he drove in his carriage from St. Cloud to Paris on the eve of his nemesis at Waterloo. Napoleon questioned Pierrot about his art and, having explained it to their mutual satisfaction, Pierrot, much encouraged, returned to prac-tise his skills among the people on whom his performances were based.

There was now greater scope for him to display these skills. The Revolution had given the players far more freedom, allowing them per-manent homes. On the Boulevard du Temple (known more familiarly as the *Boulevard du Crime*) on the Left Bank, a clutch of theatres had been erected. These specialised in mime, tight-rope walking, acrobatics, puppet shows and melodrama. Pierrot figures began performing at the Théâtre des Funambules (the latter meaning 'acrobat' or tight-rope walker'), which was formerly a dogs' circus and was now licensed sole-ly for acrobatics and mime. It was on this rough and dangerous stage that the finest of all interpreters of Pierrot was to appear. He was Jean Gaspard Deburau, nicknamed Baptiste.

Deburau was born in Bohemia in 1795. His mother was Silesian, his father Philippe was a French tumbler. Philippe had a troupe of acrobats, most of them his own children, who travelled all over Europe. Archetypal Frenchman as he now seems, Deburau did not enter France until he was eighteen (it was said that he 'spoke every language as a foreigner'). When the family were taken on at the Funambules, Deburau, then the clumsiest of them, was thrown in as a part of the deal. He worked as a stage-hand, and did not become Pierrot until after the death of his father when Deburau was thirty. Tall, thin and linen-suited (no collar now to hinder the movements of his neck) this White Clown wore instead of the straw hat of the poor or the floppy cap of the dunce, an elegant black velvet skull-cap. He used only the most basic of props: flour for his face, four candles and two out-of-tune violins. He was now no longer a clumsy figure: in a theatre of acrobats he was outstandingly agile and active. And his performance was mute – he was reported to have only ever uttered two words on stage: *Achetez salade!* in a pantomime of 1829. (His linguistic difficulties may have contributed to his silence.)

Deburau had probably first come to attention when he performed in another earlier pantomime called *Le Boeuf Enragé* with Philippe Laurent. Laurent had worked in England, and had brought back this peculiarly English form of theatre to the Funambules. The performance was seen by the influential critic, Charles Nodier, who in 1828 praised the production

and, in particular, the performances of Deburau and Laurent. So enthusiastic was Nodier that he went on to write a piece of his own for the theatre, *Le Songe d'Or* (dream of riches). By 1830, the Funambule's production of *Mother Goose* was being watched by an audience of writers and poets as well as the habitual *canaille*: the unruly crowds who packed the high galleries (the *paradis*, or gods) and who adored him. 'The *paradis*,' Richard Holmes wrote, 'hung upon his face.'

18 Contemporary drawing of Baptiste Deburau holding the stage in his hand.

Deburau's eloquence was such that if there was a noise backstage the audience would shout for silence, as if they were afraid of missing one word of his mime. Among the many who watched him were the poets Théophile Gautier and Charles Baudelaire. Baudelaire described him as 'pale as the moon, mysterious as silence, supple and mute as the serpent, thin and long as a gibbet'. Inspirer of poets, Pierrot had entered the literary world. His position was confirmed in 1832 when Jules Janin, *le prince des critiques*, published his *Histoire du Théâtre à Quatre Sous*, a work which extolled the Funambules over classical theatre, and singled out Deburau, saying of him that 'He is the instinct of the people, the spirit of the people, the life of the people'. At this point, perhaps, and at these words, Deburau began taking himself too seriously. He was, after all, only a clown.

In 1836 Philippe Laurent moved to the Cirque Olympique, leaving Deburau at centre stage in the Funambules. Consequently, his Pierrot became even more important in the pantomimes. Now much more assertive, he could even win the girl, and would hand out blows rather than receiving them. Deburau had taken over the show.

Deburau was so successful he could do no wrong. But the violence of his temperament, which gave another, uneasy, dimension to his performance, was in his own life a real danger. In 1836, when a boy insulted the clown and his wife out in the street, calling his wife a whore, Deburau retaliated by hitting out at him with his cane. He struck only once, but the boy died. Deburau was in a court as full as the Funambules would have been for any of his performances. The crowds had come, it was said, not just to witness the trial, but *to hear Deburau speak*. Deburau spoke, and was acquitted, but the tragic event was permanently to darken his act.

The show did go on, although by 1840 Deburau's health was beginning to fail and a young actor called Paul Legrand was employed to work as a double with him. Deburau died in 1846 and was much mourned. His son Jean-Charles began to play Pierrot the following year and in 1862, when the Funambules and the rest of the Boulevard du Temple were about to be demolished as a part of Baron

Haussmann's grand designs for Paris, there was a 'silent valediction' by the younger Deburau called *Pierrot's Memories*. The White Clown was dressed in black for a fitting final performance at the theatre.

Deburau's fullest tribute came eighty years later in Marcel Carné's film *Les Enfants du Paradis*, shot in wartime France with Jean-Louis Barrault as the Pierrot.. However, Deburau himself had left behind two immediate interpreters of his role, his son Charles, who followed very closely in his father's footsteps, and Legrand, who brought out the dramatic rather than the acrobatic qualities of his mentor's Pierrot, in a retrograde performance, less comic and more sentimental.

Phyllis Hartnoll has noted in her *Oxford Companion to the Theatre* how over in England Pierrot was beginning to develop a new persona, that of a 'lackadaisical, love-sick youth pining from unrequited love, and much addicted to singing mournful ballads under a full moon'.

It was in 1891 that a Deburau-esque Pierrot appeared on the English stage. He made his debut at London's Prince of Wales Theatre, in a pantomime by Michel Carré called *L'Enfant prodigue* which had been performed to great acclaim in Paris the previous year. Since the show was without words, mimed to music – that is, a French pantomime – it's difficult from such a distance to assess its appeal, but the word generally used of the piece is 'haunting'. The Prodigal Son was a much-explored theme in France at the time, and in this version Monsieur – and Madame – Pierrot mourn over their wayward child. Pierrot has now found a wife and a child (the latter played by a woman, Félicia Mallet in Paris, and in England by Jane May). The show and its music hall imitations proved as popular in England as in France, and entertainers took up the name 'pierrot' (partly, it has been suggested, because of the word's happy seaside association with 'pier'). Suddenly, and rather inexplicably Pierrot, who had been something of a loner, spawned entire troupes of his kind. Among the first was singer and banjo player Clifford Essex's Pierrot Banjo Team. Essex, with Joe Morley, banjo-player, and James Blakeley, comedian, along with Miss Dewhirste, harmonium, performed on house-boats at Henley Regatta and, in 1892, at Cowes Regatta, where they did a Command

Performance for the Prince of Wales. As a result, the future Edward VII gave them permission to call themselves the Royal Pierrots.

There were Royal Pierrots in Weymouth by 1906, though they belonged to one of Will Catlin's growing number of troupes, found mainly on the east coast (but for some reason also in Weymouth). Catlin's Pierrots were the second company to be so honoured, being summoned by royal command to visit Ruthin Castle when Edward VII was staying there. Unlike Clifford Essex, Scarborough-based Catlin did not allow women into his troupes. In *Beside the Seaside*, Clarkson Rose explained the reasoning behind Catlin's ban.

> Every artiste had clauses in his contract requiring him to walk in full make-up and Pierrot costume from his 'digs' to the pitch; that, if he was married, his wife should not come near the pitch; and that he should not be seen arm-in-arm in public with any female. Such stipulations were quite usual, for the Pierrots were the glamour boys of the time, and nothing could be allowed which might affect their appeal to the fair sex.

A born entrepreneur, Catlin was one of the first managers to use advertising, handing out picture postcards of the local troupe to holiday-makers on their arrival. The visitors would then send the cards back home, and so more and more people would come to know about Catlin's pierrots. The troupes performed three times daily, 'weather and tide permitting', and five times on Bank Holidays.

The swift rise to popularity of these pale-faced creatures – who sometimes called themselves 'white coons' – led to a decline in the prominence of the blacked-up 'Nigger Minstrels', who had been a staple of the Victorian sands. A single American minstrel performer, T.D.Rice, had appeared at the old Surrey Theatre in London in 1836 and was an immediate success, one which was much imitated. Following the emancipation of slaves in the southern states of America, many more performers appeared – some of them genuine black men, the rest requiring applications of burnt cork. They

19 Catlin's Pierrots in Weymouth.

sounded different too, playing the banjo, an instrument previously unheard in England, along with the tambourine, cornet, concertina, strings – and bones. Troupes like Uncle Lynn's and Jack Hylton's continued to appear in Weymouth (the latter on the Nothe), but they were no longer the main attraction. *Variety Theatre* described the upstarts who displaced them.

> Pierrot became the order of the day. The tasteful white costumes of loose blouse, ornamented with pom-pom, the equally loose pantaloons, the natty shoe, and the black silk handkerchief which wound artistically round the head, and tied tastefully at the side, and surmounted by the conical white hat fairly 'caught on'.

What came to be perhaps the most famous Pierrot troupe had its beginnings in Weymouth when Edwin Adeler, son of a Presbyterian minister, joined forces with W.G.Sutton. In 1894 they performed together on the town's promenade, with a hired piano mounted on a trolley (and a hired pianist to go with it). The pair then moved on to Harrogate, where they became full Pierrots, whitening up with zinc and lard, as was the custom. Thus began the Adeler-Sutton Pierrots, who had more than fifteen pitches by the early 1900s. (At first these pierrots, too were all-male, but later each Adeler-Sutton company acquired a token pierrette.)

Pierrots seem to have rapidly become a fixture in Weymouth, with the official guide for 1913 confidently remarking that 'the ubiquitous pierrot, is of course, to be found on the sands'. Yet while the 'White Coons' were overtaking the 'Nigger' troupes, one very elaborate black and white minstrel show provided a unique performance on February 7 1910. That afternoon, H.M.S. Dreadnought, lying off Portland, received a telegram informing Admiral Sir William May, Commander-in-Chief of the Home Fleet, that Prince Makalen of Abyssinia, would be shortly arriving in Weymouth with his interpreter and suite.

Given only half an hour to prepare, the officers responded swiftly, donning full dress and arranging for a guard of honour and a launch to greet the unexpected guests. Weymouth's Mayor and Corporation met the party at the station. Reporting on the occasion, the *Daily Mirror* said that

> All the princes wore vari-coloured sashes as turbans, set off with diamond aigrettes, white gibbah tunics, over which were cast rich flowing robes, and round their necks were suspended gold chains and jewelled necklaces.
>
> Their faces were coloured a deep brown with a specially prepared powder, and half-hidden under dark false beards and moustaches, while, except in the case of the lady, their hair was dyed black and crisply curled.

Under the disguises, supplied by a London costumier, were the artist Duncan Grant, two friends – and a moustachioed Virginia Stephen (better known as the novelist Virginia Woolf). Her brother Adrian acted as interpreter, deepening his voice and 'improvising in a mixture of broken Virgil, the Abyssinians responding with "Bunga-Bunga"', as Woolf's biographer Hermione Lee described it. Adrian Stephen and the arch-conspirator and ace practical joker Horace de Vere Cole (who acted the role of Herbert Cholmondely, Foreign Office attaché) were the instigators of the hoax. 'He did little else during his lifetime, but he did once contribute to the gaiety of nations', Virginia's nephew Quentin Bell wrote in 1983 in his introduction to Stephens's book on the affair.

The party boarded the ship to the rousing sounds of the Anthem of Zanzibar, the closest tune the bandmaster could find to the Abyssinian National Anthem. They were shown round the ship by the Stephens's cousin, Commander William Fisher, who (to his later fury and chagrin) failed to recognise his relatives – despite the facts that Virginia was in unconvincing drag, and Adrian Stephen was '6 ft.5in. in his socks'.

The whole plan, hastily conceived, could easily have failed. As Hermione Lee has written, its success depended, 'to a breath-taking degree on the general ignorance of all things African'. This certainly seems to have been the case. It was a wonder the tricksters were not exposed. Duncan Grant's moustache began to peel off at some point, and one of the princes slipped and nearly landed in the sea, which would have washed away his face paint. The 'Dreadnought Hoax' could be regarded as a subversive act, pricking the pomposity of the naval command, or else as the kind of prank from which only the well-connected would emerge unscathed.

Certainly, it caused great amusement in Weymouth. At the new Pavilion Theatre the music hall comedian Mr. Medley Barrett was met with great enthusiasm when he sang this song (to the tune of 'The Girl I Left Behind Me'):

When I went on board a Dreadnought ship,
Though I looked just like a costermonger
They said I was an Abyssinian prince,
Because I shouted 'Bunga-Bunga'.

Although efforts had been made to keep the incident a secret, 'Bunga-Bunga' was also shouted at Dreadnought's crew when they ventured into Weymouth. Questions were asked in Parliament and the whole affair was reported in the *Daily Mirror* (tipped off, Adrian Stephen suspected, by de Vere Cole). A *Mirror* cartoon which predicted 'what will happen next time some genuine Eastern princes visit a British man o' war', proved surprisingly accurate as Virginia Woolf confirmed in 1940.

> About a week or two later the real Emperor of Abyssinia arrived in London. He complained that wherever he went in the street boys ran after him calling out Bunga Bunga. And when he asked the First Lord of the Admiralty whether he might visit the Channel Fleet, Mr. McKenna replied that he regretted to inform his Majesty that it was quite impossible.

20 Cartoon in Daily Mirror, *February 1910.*

Another historic moment for Weymouth had come in 1894 when the first concert party was held in the resort. The performers were Carlton Frederick's company, the Fez-Olympians, of whom only a photograph has been traced.

Frederick however went on to run other companies, such as Merrymakers and Les Vivandières. Among other early concert parties was Ballard Brown's Entertainers, initially like his rivals an all-male troupe, dressed in white flannel trousers, red blazers and straw hats. (A postcard of around 1913 shows the troupe's leader solo, in kilt and trappings entitled 'Mr. Ballard Brown in Scotland's Glory'.) By 1905 Ballard Brown and his party were a mixed troupe, 'four men and two ladies', who appeared on the beach's Concert Platform in its inaugural season – and as a special favour were allowed fifty deckchairs for the opening night. (In 1906 Weymouth's councillors agreed that this portable stage 'should be styled The Sea View Concert Platform'. Only

21 Fez-Olympians concert party in Weymouth.

22 Concert Platform on the beach in the 1900s.

the Council persisted in using this misleading title. Those performing had their backs to the water, and the audience's view was obscured by the stage.) The platform was positioned at the harbour end of the sands, opposite the modern Marks & Spencer store. At first it was little more than an outdoor stage; later it provided the artistes with more shelter.

Ballard Brown proved a rather truculent and awkward character, often behind with his rent, who demanded new fixtures – and complained about the behaviour of the tides. In 1906 the council accepted Mr. Catlin's rival tender of £100, and for a few years the two companies alternated on the beach platform. Mostly, though, Ballard Brown was on the platform, returning to resume his place there in 1919 after the wartime closure of the stage. By 1921 he had graduated to the Alexandra Gardens.

And Pierrot? Once at the seaside, Pierrot became a shadow of himself, a lunar creature wilting under the hot August sun, performing in silly bobbling pompoms, his identity almost gone. Yet the melancholy remained, if for different reasons.

In Weymouth, pierrots – and pierrettes – played their routines on the wide, wooden green-and-white portable Concert Platform, open to the Esplanade. The players wore loose-fitting costumes, white with black pompons for pierrettes, and the reverse for the pierrots. Heavily made up (though not with whitened faces) the women wore short full skirts and the men baggy trousers and pointed hats – Pierrot had once again become a fool. A gregarious crew, 'they sang and danced with gusto and their feet made satisfying thumps on the wooden floor, which shook', as Sheila Milton remembers. No mime was used, and the only real link with Pierrot as he had been, other than their parodic costume, was their residual sadness, that of people no longer young but still obliged to make a precarious and arduous living by performing two or three times a day. As if to stress this aspect of their character, their subjection, they were heavily ruffed.

In their turn the pierrots were losing out to the concert parties, whose shows involved changes of costume and were a little more elaborate. Val Vaux (real name William Valentine Whitehouse-Vaux) and his company, the Vaudesques, had a vaudeville show on Weymouth beach during the 1920s and 1930s. Vaudeville was the American word for a concert party – and also alliterated nicely with

BALLARD BROWNS ENTERTAINERS.
OLYMPIA. WEYMOUTH ~ SEASON. 1913.

23 Ballard Brown and his troupe.

the leader's name. They too performed each season in the oblong wooden pavilion, box-like and sturdy, which formed the Concert Platform. By now there was a trellis at the back of the stage where the performers entered and left, while a narrow passage behind served as their dressing-rooms. The audience were provided with (cheaper) upright metal chairs or with the more comfortable deckchairs.

Margaret Morris still remembers the company well. She describes Val Vaux's wife, Jenny, whose stage name was Ruby Lea, as a sharp woman who kept her eye on the cash. She was the troupe's bottler, collecting the money in a wooden box with a handle. Dawn Gould too has memories of Ruby Lea as an indomitable character. 'She was 100% Tartar and ruled with a rod of iron.' The troupe's dancer was called Tilly Dorane.

Because she lived in Weymouth, Dawn was not allowed to enter Val Vaux's talent competitions, a feature of his show. At a very early age, however, she managed to bypass this rule. 'I sneaked on at two and a half and won a prize for "Let's All Sing Like the Birdies Sing" ' – which must have been one in the eye for Ruby Lea.

24 *Pierrot troupe on the Concert Platform.*

25 *Val Vaux's Vaudesques.* TOP ROW: *Sidney, Reg Graham, Val Vaux, Tony Alden.* BOTTOM ROW: *Ruby Lea, Tilly Dorane, unknown.*

As was customary with concert parties, the performance fell into two parts. In the first, the women wore pompoms, short skirts and bandeaux. The men too were dressed in white as pierrots.

Later on they seem to have introduced a ticket booth. Pamela Haines, whose aunt Edith Wombwell was the cashier – Pamela was sometimes allowed free admission – can recall their opening number, which went like this:

> *How do you do, do dee do do do*
> *How do you do do do*
> *We're glad to see you here and rather*
> *Hope you're in the pink and how's your father!*

They sang and danced to the accompaniment of a piano on the left of the stage. (The pianist, thought to be the cleverest and most talented of the group, was called Charlie.) Joyce Otter, taken to see them in 1934 on a Sunday School treat, remembers that they sang 'all

26 Val Vaux's troupe performing as pierrots.

the old songs' from before the First World War, songs such as 'Just like the Ivy, I'll Cling to You'. They were a colourful sight.

The second part was more sophisticated, chiaroscuro, and influenced by the contemporary craze for the top-hat-and-tail films of dancing partners Fred Astaire and Ginger Rogers. Night-time performances were more formal and evening dress was worn.

Val Vaux's troupe was popular, playing all summer long. A carnival night was included in their repertoire, when they would throw gifts and streamers at the audience. Yet despite their popularity, times could be hard. So much was dependent on the weather. In October 1927 for instance, Val Vaux who was applying to hire the Concert Platform at an unincreased rate the next summer, asked for a rebate for 1927 as it had been a 'wet season'. The Borough Council declined.

There was also competition from the performers at the Alexandra Gardens Concert Hall, a theatre built in 1924 and set in gardens closer to the harbour. (In its turn, competition for the Concert Hall came from the Pavilion Theatre, a charming Edwardian building with Tea

27 *Concert Platform on the beach in the 1930s.*

Room and skating-rink, erected in 1908 on reclaimed land by the pier.) In further discussion of their plans for the 1928 season the Council agreed to hire a string of concert parties for the Hall. These included The Piccadilly Follies, Frivolity, Bubbles, Rogues and Irresponsibles, some of them quite famous companies. Rival pierrot troupes performed there, such as 'the Pierrots in Plus Fours (all men)' who appeared in 1931. Not all of them, though, could have felt as light-hearted as their names – and probably not all of them actually fulfilled their bookings – due to 'a year of depression in Concert Parties'. In fact there was much debate amongst the councillors as to whether the Council should make up any losses, but the feeling was generally against such an approach. It was further agreed to hire George Hay's Concert Party for a longer stretch of twelve weeks, along with an accompanying Octette. Hay's company consisted of twelve artistes – Miss Phyllis Wright, Mr. Reginald Alderton, Miss Jean String, Mr. Bertram Colmer (Baritone), first and second comedians, comedienne and soubrette entertainers, three girl dancers – and Mr. George Hay at

28 Alexandra Gardens Concert Hall photographed by Edwin Seward.

the piano. The period between the wars was the heyday of such companies, and as can be seen many of them appeared in Weymouth.

Very few of these performers returned after the Second World War had ended. The rolls of barbed wire across Weymouth's beaches seemed like a wavy rusted line dividing the high tide of seaside entertainment from the slow decline of the post-war years. Weymouth's pierrots never came back. Perhaps, like the anonymous voices below, they had a premonition of their fate.

> *We're the last of Britain's pierrots, two optimistic heroes*
> *We've played every beach from Blundell Sands to Bude,*
> *To an audience all sitting with their crosswords or their knitting,*
> *And to small boys who made noises which to say the least were rude.*
>
> *One Bank Holiday at Sandown, the rain it simply ran down*
> *But we carried on completely in a daze.*
> *And at Weymouth our soprano, caught her head in the piano,*
> *Still we got it out at Walton-on-the-Naze.*

One Whit-Monday up at Clacton we put a brand new act on
We performed to two small children with their dolls
Tho' they heard our opening chorus they hadn't much time for us
'Cos they thought they'd come to see the 'Fol-de-Rols'.

So just spare a thought for pierrot when the temperature's at zero
As he sings through mists and rain in early May.
He feels really appalling for there's a gap in the tarpaulin
And the wind blows up his trousers on 'The Road to Mandalay'.

We've been pushed into the background by the progress of events,
For on the beach at Brighton where we used to pitch our tents,
They've built a place for 'Ladies' and another one for 'Gents'
For pierrot isn't wanted anymore.

29 Interior of the old Pavilion Theatre (Edwin Seward).

Pierrot has vanished now from England, except as a sentimental souvenir, a floppy pink-cheeked doll. Shrewdly, he has returned to France, where he always fared better, and where he has been an active presence in twentieth century European music, mime, painting and ballet.

Yet one of his distant descendants can still be seen on the English sands. For Pierrot survives in the Punch & Judy shows – in the guise of Joey the Clown.

30 Joey the Clown by Frank Edmonds.

Joey the Clown

The business of the Weymouth stage is well conducted by Mr. Hughes. The house is elegantly fitted up, and the performers are frequently of the first order of merit. The best comedians from the London and Bath theatres, frequently exhibit their talents here, particularly during the residence of the royal family. The boxes are sufficiently large to accommodate 400 spectators.

Guide to Weymouth, 1811

PITT
What curious structure do I see outside, sir?
KING
It's but a stage, a type of all the world.

Thomas Hardy, *The Dynasts*

31 *Joseph Grimaldi, the original Joey the Clown.*

I N A PERIOD WHEN new theatres were being built all over the country, Weymouth was not to be left behind. The town possessed its own playhouse as early as 1770, and this was shown on the Weymouth street plan in Hutchins' *History of Dorset* (first edition) in 1774. Among Weymouth Library's impressive collection of playbills for the theatre there is one from 1770 for the penultimate performance of the popular play *Jane Shore*, 'a tragedy'. This was followed by an entertainment called *The Devil to Pay, or the Wives Metamorphos'd*, and an epilogue featuring Mr. Palmer 'Riding on an ASS' – a dramatic mix characteristic of the time. The performance took place in what was described as 'the New Theatre in Weymouth'.

Although occupying the same site – on the Esplanade, near the corner of Augusta Place and of the older Bond Street and extending as far back as what is now New Street – it was a very different building from its more famous successor. In the 1780s Richard Hughes, who already owned or managed playhouses at Plymouth and Exeter, also took charge of the Weymouth theatre. With the help of local architect James Hamilton, he was soon carrying out drastic alterations to the little structure. The *New Weymouth Guide* refers to it in 1798, describing 'the many improvements the *Theatre* has undergone, by Mr. Hamilton the Architect, which is under the management of Mr. Hughes the owner, who at a vast expense had enlarged and ornamented it in an excellent, and elegant style. The boxes and gallery are on a circular construction; the boxes in particular, are rendered so commodious, that they will contain nearly 400 people, and the manner in which they are fitted up, are equal to the Theatre Royal, in London.'

A painting of the outside of the theatre, made by visitor Francis Justice in 1796, shows the canopied entrance on the Esplanade, erected when King George III began to spend his summers in the town. The auditorium itself was down a passageway from the canopied door on the left-hand side of the present building at No.10 Augusta Place. The theatre was enclosed by houses, including the one which forms the frontage of No.10. By 1802, as a sketch by a member of the company James Winston shows, the triangular-shaped canopy had gone, though the door behind it remained – but was no longer necessary, as a new entrance had been built at No.10 surmounted by the Royal Arms.

At some point after 1802, an entrance was built to the side in Bond Street which became the main entrance, and can still be seen. The door opens on to a sweep of low, wide stairs leading up to the auditorium in a position backing on to what is now its rear wall in New Street. A second set of boxes was added in 1825.

The theatre remained in the hands of the Hughes family until the 1830s, after which a series of managers tried to revive its flagging fortunes. Like Weymouth itself, the theatre had never quite recovered from the departure of the last members of the royal family in 1817. Closure finally came in 1859, by which time trade had actually picked up a little, due partly to the crowd-pulling presence in Portland Roads of Brunel's steamship, the *Great Eastern*, brought in for repair after an explosion. It was rumoured that a replacement theatre was about to be

32 *Theatre Royal in 1802 by actor James Winston.*

built – and not before time, commented the local correspondent of the *Era*. 'A more miserable little box than the present building can hardly be conceived, although it is the time-honoured temple of the Muse wherein his Majesty George the Third derived amusement in many a gladsome hour.'

A playbill gives the last night of the last season as October 3rd, at which the Town Band played, though performances actually went on into December, as the *Southern Times* proudly proclaimed:

> Theatre Royal, Esplanade, Weymouth. Saturday, November 26, 1859, and every Evening during next week under the management of Mr. H. Walker. Positively the last night but six. Unprecedented Novelties, Unrivalled Feats, performed every evening by the most Talented, Classical, and Accomplished Artistes of the Present Day. Mid-Day Performances, doors open at half past One o'clock precisely – performance commences at two. Last Mid-Day Representation will take place on Friday, Dec. 3rd.

The theatre seems to have closed for good on December 4th, though the new Theatre Royal in St. Nicholas Street did not open until 1865. In the meantime, from 1860 to 1863, the players performed on a portable stage. In 1863 they also performed at Burdon's Assembly Rooms, and in 1864 at the Victoria Assembly Rooms. The new theatre was known at first as the 'New Concert Hall' or, 'New Music Hall' and was a converted Congregational chapel. Its short life lasted until 1893.

Astonishingly, though the Theatre Royal's replacement and name-sake in St. Nicholas Street has gone entirely – its arch lingering forlornly on for a while, awkwardly decorating a car park – the older theatre remains, hidden inside a nightclub, with a now-restored frieze of cherubs and vines around the walls. It is strange to be able to visit the room where the King and his courtiers had so often sat, and where Joey Grimaldi, Mrs. Siddons and the young, unknown Edmund Kean had all appeared. The room which was the King's antechamber is still there

33 Restored frieze in the auditorium of the old Theatre Royal.

too, and also the cellar (now a bar) which would have housed the actors' dressing-room and the stage machinery.

Down in the cellar, the outline of the huge fireplace which provided both heat and cooking facilities for the actors is still visible, and a boxed-off space against the New Street wall is where stairs once led to up the back of the stage. This cellar is at ground level on the New Street side, and probably served as stables for the horses and carriages of important visitors. (Until recently there was a large peg on the ground floor which was most likely used for stacking saddles.)

Another cellar acted as a store. Underneath this part of Weymouth is a maze of tunnels, emerging from the theatre and leading towards the centre of the town. They may have been used in troubled times to provide safe passage for the King; they were also the site of brothels, and routes for the smugglers who were rife in the years when smuggling was still a national sport.

The theatre is tiny, although it was said to seat around 400 people (sitting packed as tightly as sardines on narrow backless benches). Candle-lit and crowded, it must often have been unbearably hot. The auditorium was U shaped, with a sunken pit (boarded up in 1853) and boxes which ringed the entire U at ground level. Above the boxes was a gallery which could hold eighty people.

The maximum measurement of the building was reckoned to be only forty by thirty-nine feet – though what it lacked in width and length it made up for in height. In his *Balnea*, G.S.Carey claimed that it was 'in the shape of a wig-box and not much bigger'. Actor James Winston noted that the stage was 'unusually small' but that the wings, a new improvement of 1802, could hold eight changes of scenery. The actress Fanny Kemble (Mrs. Siddons' niece) called it 'a perfect doll's play-house' when she appeared there in 1831 during her first provincial tour. This pocket playhouse, however, acquired its grand title when it was patronised by King George III, his Queen and some of their many children during the family's first visit to Weymouth in 1789. In the second edition of his Dorset history, 1803, John Hutchins describes how Mr. Hughes 'during the King's first visit, by proper attention to the duties of his office, was not only honoured by frequent commands, but had his play-house distinguished by the

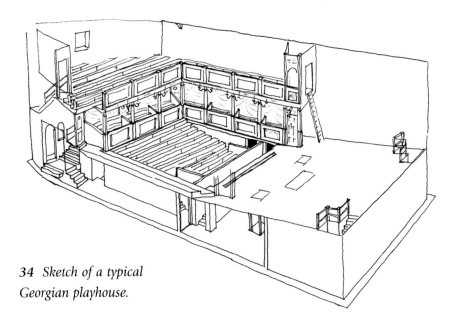

34 Sketch of a typical Georgian playhouse.

dignity of a Theatre Royal; nor was his Majesty more negligent of the manager when he afterwards honoured Weymouth with his royal presence'.

All this was hard work for Richard Hughes to maintain. London bookseller James Lackington observed on a visit in 1791 that Hughes had scarcely a moment to himself, what with managing both the Weymouth and Exeter companies, performing six or even eight times a week and painting the stage scenery. He also had 'a large expensive family (nine children)'. Lackington added that the theatre had been rebuilt 'about four years since'.

A poster of 1791 advertises the venue under its smart new title and proclaims (as do many subsequent playbills) *Vivat Rex et Regina'*. Royal patronage enabled the theatre to increase its prices for boxes by a shilling in 1792, and even to offer season tickets. The King was a keen theatre-goer – though he didn't care much for the works of Shakespeare – and despite his nickname, 'Farmer George' and his notoriously frugal habits, he was a very cultured man. The King's Library – which now forms the centrepiece of the entrance to the British Library – came from his personal collection, and George III was instrumental too in the founding of the Royal Academy. So he would naturally wish to visit the theatre when he went to Weymouth.

In the 1801 season the Royal Family went to the Theatre Royal fifty-one times in thirteen weeks, a 'golden harvest' for Mr. Hughes. In fact they became quite involved with the company, on one occasion making arrangements for the actress Mrs. Lee to go into a sanatorium when they noticed the severity of her cough during a play. The King and Queen also gave their patronage to many benefit performances, from which all the money raised was given to one or two members of the cast or their families. In Weymouth, benefits were used for other purposes too. On October 11 1798 there was one in aid of the widows and orphans of the Battle of the Nile when *The Heir at Law* and *The Village Lawyer* were performed.

The King and his family were seated in the Royal Box (boxes held about twenty people) directly facing the stage and beneath a red canopy edged with gold. This feature was described in 1791 by the *Dublin Chronicle* : 'A beautiful canopy had been put up in the centre front box, of crimson silk, with gold fringe, the inside of the curtain, or vallens, lined with pink, and the top with white Persian; the canopy supported by four pillars.'

Despite such trappings, the Royal Family sat on benches like every-one else (they practised, as historian Ronald Good wrote, a kind of 'democratic domesticity') and their attendants stood behind them. Mr. Hughes had intended to make a more splendid royal box, but the King would not allow it. Instead, three rows were simply cordoned off for the Court's exclusive use. 'God Save the King', soon to become the National Anthem, was played at every performance attended by the mild monarch.

The boxes could not have been quite as uncomfortable as they sound in contemporary accounts. The story goes that no less an actor than Robert William Elliston, future lessee and patent holder of the Drury Lane Theatre, found the King asleep in his box one evening around six o'clock (as he was also apt to be during performances). He had taken shelter there from a shower of rain. The performance (Elliston's Benefit) was due to begin in half an hour, and the frantic actor snatched up a fiddle and played 'God Save the King'. This had the required effect: the King awoke, and stayed on for the performance, sending for the Queen and princesses to join him.

Another play-goer was Fanny Burney, in her capacity as Assistant Keeper of the Wardrobe to Queen Charlotte. Already known as the author of two novels, *Evelina* and *Cecilia*, Fanny found her current employment tedious beyond belief. In particular she hated the rigorous and fussy etiquette, which involved much standing about. Even more inconveniently, although she was short-sighted, she was not allowed to wear her glasses at court. And perhaps worst of all, her superior, Mrs. Schwellenberg, who had come over from Mecklenburg-Strelitz with Queen Charlotte on the latter's wedding, proved to be so intimidating that she even alarmed her royal mistress. Fanny was accustomed to the artistic circles at her family home in Leicester

35 Fanny Burney

Square, and had accepted the robe-keeping position in the hope of furthering her father Charles's career (he had ambitions to become the King's Master of Music). In her famous diary, which must have been a welcome distraction from her duties, Miss Burney described the Royal party's first visit to the Weymouth Theatre. She was certainly not over-impressed by the experience.

Thursday July 16th [1789]. Yesterday we all went to the theatre. The King has taken the centre front box for himself, and family, and attendants. The side boxes are too small. The Queen ordered places for Miss Planta and me, which are in the front row of a box next but one to the Royals. Thus, in our case, our want of rank to be in their public suite gives us better seats than those <u>high</u> enough to stand behind them!

…'Tis a pretty little theatre, but its entertainment was quite in the barn style: a mere medley – songs, dances, imitations – and all very bad. But Lord Chesterfield, who is here, and who seems chief director, promises all will be better.

Lord Chesterfield must have moved swiftly, as Miss Burney cheerfully praised the next performance she attended. Just over a week later on July 25th she wrote that *The Commissary* (adapted from Molière's play *Le Bourgeois Gentilhomme*) made her 'laugh quite immoderately…'

Now, as the King began to make regular visits, the little theatre rapidly became fashionable, attracting more illustrious audiences and players.

The appellation 'royal' was not just given to the theatre. A playbill of 1798 for a lavish production of *Castle Spectre* by M.G.Lewis (better known as 'Monk' Lewis, Gothic novelist) advises that tickets may be had at Mr. Rolls, 'Hosiers, Glover, etc.' By 1802, tickets can still be obtained from Mr. Rolls, but he is now described as 'Glover and Breeches Maker to His Majesty, and Pantaloon Maker to His R.H. the Duke of Cumberland, Augusta Place adjoining the Theatre...'

The Theatre Royal features in Thomas Hardy's novel of the Napoleonic wars, *The Trumpet-Major*, published in 1880, when the lovers Anne Garland and Bob Loveday pay a visit to the playhouse 'in their gayest clothes, to do justice to the places taken'. Their outfits are fully described by Hardy, who had researched the period in the British Museum in preparation for writing the work, which was his only historical novel. Hardy bound his manuscript notes into a book which is still on display in the Dorset County Museum, and is known as 'The Trumpet-Major Notebook'. It is a unique miscellany of costumes, customs, royal doings, battles and beacons. Hardy used his research material both for the novel and later for his epic drama *The Dynasts*.

In *The Trumpet-Major*, despite the hot August weather, Anne and Bob are well wrapped up for their theatre-going. The grand occasion requires Bob to sport two fancy waistcoats, pantaloons and a new pair of boots. Anne, meanwhile, is wearing a muslin dress 'with the waist under the arms', a plaited straw hat – and a fur-trimmed coat. It is a 'King's night' and the royal family take their central seats, accompanied by 'a crowd of powdered and glittering personages of fashion'.

The star of that evening's performance, Hardy noted, was Jack Bannister, a well-regarded actor who had been trained by David Garrick. The play was George Colman's comedy *Heir-at-Law* in which Bannister played the Doctor, and which was followed by the opera *No Song, No Supper*. Both are included in a list in 'The Trumpet-Major Notebook' of the dramas performed at the Theatre Royal during those exalted nights.

Such details always fascinated Hardy, who was a keen theatre-goer (and eminently fond of actresses). One evening in the winter of 1866–7 he even played a walk-on role in a pantomime at Covent Garden entitled *Ali-Baba and the Forty Thieves; or, Harlequin and the Genii of the Arabian Nights!* Hardy was very preoccupied with the theatre while he was writing *The Trumpet-Major*, because at the same time he was working on a stage adaptation of another of his novels, *Far From the Madding Crowd*. The play, called *The Mistress of the Farm*, was his first attempt at play-writing. It's surely no coincidence that much of *The Trumpet-Major* too was shaped by its author into a further form of drama – a derivative of the Commedia dell'Arte known as the *harlequinade.*

The harlequinade took place only after the main part of the bill – often a serious play – was over. Performances were long and arduous for the actors, who might appear in both play and harlequinade, plus any other dramatic piece which preceded them.(An evening at the theatre in Georgian times meant exactly what it said.) Harlequin, who of course gave his name to this new hybrid, was the best-known Commedia figure in England (as he was in France) when the genre first began to appear. The harlequinade was a fusion between the dumb-shows of the Parisian fairs and the contemporary burlesque dramas in which Harlequin took on a variety of personalities while managing to keep his own persona. Even after he lost his major role in the performances, Harlequin continued to give his name to the genre and also to contribute to the titles of the dramas. Other Commedia characters featured as well, including Columbine who, with Harlequin as her lover, triumphantly escaped adversity by means of magic and some spectacular stage machinery. Music and mime were used, characters were transformed and appeared in fantastic guises in this highly popular dramatic form.

Hardy's uses of the harlequinade are more integral to his novel than John Cowper Powys's conjurings of Commedia figures in *Weymouth Sands* – though the fact that both writers employ these characters seems to suggest just how closely in England Commedia and the harlequinade had become linked to the seaside. In *The Trumpet-Major* Anne Garland is a Columbine-like figure, fair ('very fair, in a poetic sense') and flirtatious. She is 'graceful and slender' and wears 'a white handkerchief to cover her white neck'.

Anne has three lovers, two of them brothers. John Loveday, the trumpet-major of the title, is a pale and serious Pierrot, a Pierrot with none of the clown in him. His brother Bob is a dark-faced, restless Harlequin, who loves to dress like a dandy, as he does on his visit with Anne to the Theatre Royal, looking 'the perfection of a beau in the dog-days'. Like any Harlequin worth his salt, sailor Bob acts with great courage and agility, eluding the press-gang who corner him in his father's mill by deftly manipulating the building's chains, hoists and trap-doors in a re-working of 'Harlequin's Leap' in the old drama.

> The foremost pursuers arrived just in time to see Captain Bob's legs and shoe-buckles vanishing through the trap-door in the joists overhead, his person having been whirled up by the machinery like any bag of flour…

Such dashing deeds lead Anne to choose Bob rather than John Loveday. She also resists the advances of Festus Derriman, the nephew and likely heir of the local landowner. Festus takes the role of the Captain in the harlequinade: he is a drunken and cowardly braggart, with a bad-tempered face 'like a turnip lantern'. He is up

36 Columbine-like Anne Garland, in a drawing by Arthur Hopkins for the first edition of The Trumpet-Major, *1880.*

to all sorts of tricks, feigning a fit to encapture Anne, and affecting courage only when he knows himself to be safely out of danger. His uncle Benjy is a regular Pantaloon, in Dorset terms a 'scram blue-vinnied gallicrow' (a puny and mouldy scarecrow). He is notoriously tight-fisted, and obsessed with protecting his wealth. Like Pantaloon, too, he has a soft spot for the novel's Columbine, ultimately bequeathing his manor house to Anne rather than to the unpleasant Festus.

Anne thus becomes an heiress and is also reunited with Bob, unexpectedly home from the sea. Once again, Harlequin has won Columbine's hand (while Festus join forces with the young actress Matilda Johnson). In the true Pierrot tradition, John has failed romantically. He is last seen at the very end of the novel, in the flickering light of a candle held by his father, going off to fight in the Peninsular War.

> …with a farewell smile he turned on the door-stone, backed by the black night; and in another moment he had plunged into the darkness, the ring of his smart step dying away upon the bridge as he joined his companions-in-arms, and went off to blow his trumpet till silenced for ever upon one of the bloody battle-fields of Spain.

The Weymouth theatre also has a part in Hardy's short story 'A Committee-Man of "the Terror"' when the Committee-Man and his reluctant escort go to see Mr. S.Kemble as Captain Absolute in

37 John Loveday's last farewell.

Sheridan's comedy *The Rivals*. Stephen Kemble was a member of the illustrious theatrical family. His more accomplished sister, Sarah – better known as Mrs. Siddons – was another Weymouth player. The distinguished actress happened to be in Weymouth at the same time as the Royal party, holidaying with her husband and 'a sweet child' for the sake of her health. Her acting was much admired by the King who was already a fan of hers, but less unreservedly so by Fanny Burney who, on meeting her at a gathering at the Royal Lodge in Windsor Park, had found her conversation 'formal, sententious, calm, and dry'. A noted tragedienne, Mrs. Siddons appeared at the Theatre Royal as Rosalind in *As You Like It*. It was reported that 'All the world, (i.e.) the <u>Weymouth</u> world, went to see Mrs. Siddons in <u>trowsers</u>'. Miss Burney, however, remained unimpressed by this bravura performance. 'I must own my admiration for her confined to her tragic powers; and there it is raised so high that I feel mortified, in a degree, to see her so much fainter attempts and success in comedy.' She was not the only member of an audience to feel dismay, as Victor J. Adams relates in his essay 'Weymouth Theatricals':

> The tale went round that Mrs. Wells, the actress displaced by Mrs. Siddons, went one night into a box when Mrs. Siddons was performing a comic part and sobbed and cried so loudly that she attracted the attention of the whole house. When people crowded round to hear the cause of her distress – "Do you think I have no tender feelings?" the actress sobbed, "Sure none but brutes could sit and see Mrs. Siddons play, without shedding floods of tears!"

However, when Mrs. Siddons appeared a few days later as Lady Townley in Vanbrugh's *The Provok'd Husband* she earned Fanny Burney's whole-hearted approval: 'Mrs. Siddons, in her looks, and the tragic part, was exquisite,' she wrote. This superb performance was achieved despite the fact that the Royal party was late back after a trip to Lulworth Castle, which meant that the audience – and performers –

38 Sarah Siddons by George Romney.

were kept waiting. Relations between the two women must have improved even further, as in the 1794–5 season at the Theatre Royal, Drury Lane, Mrs. Siddons actually appeared in Miss Burney's tragedy, *Edwy and Elgiva*. This was not a success. Siddons' first biographer, the poet Thomas Campbell, described its first night:

Miss Burney was peculiarly unfortunate in bringing bishops into her tragedy. At that time there was a liquor much in popular use, called Bishop: it was a sort of negus or punch, I believe … when jolly fellows met at a tavern, the first order to the waiter was, *to bring in the Bishop.* Unacquainted with the language of taverns, Miss Burney made her King exclaim, in an early scene, *'Bring in the Bishop!'* and the summons filled the audience with as much hilarity as if they had drank of the exhilarating liquor.

In 1791, some time before this theatrical disaster, Fanny Burney retired from her wearisome court role. So she was regrettably not present to comment on the appearance at the Theatre Royal of the great clown, Joseph Grimaldi. Grimaldi, with red-orange flashes across his whitened cheeks, with his baggy trousers and his cockerel crest – a parody of foppish male fashions – was a well-known performer. While he was appearing in the town, Grimaldi was believed to have given an 'impromptu song' in praise of seaside Weymouth. The song was passed on to W.Bowles Barrett around 1883 by 'a resident medical practitioner, then aged 80 years or upwards'. This is how the old doctor remembered the words:

> *Many towns have I oft heard extolled*
> *For their cleanliness, beauty and trade,*
> *Their churches and buildings so old,*
> *And their streets so completely well made.*
>
> *But the place of all places for me,*
> *Is Weymouth, so handsome and gay,*
> *Where you sniff the salt air of the sea,*
> *And drive your complaints all away.*
>
> *On the grand esplanade you may walk*
> *Where Beauty and Fashion combine;*
> *There you hear the Nobility talk,*
> *Lord, Chancellor, Duke and Divine.*
>
> *On the sands see the curricles roll,*
> *Gay chariots and tandems beside,*
> *And ladies – between pole and pole –*
> *By the help of two men take a ride.*
>
> *There are Bathing Machines in a row,*
> *That you ride in to pickle your skin,*
> *(Kept by Scriven, Ford, Saxon & Co.),*
> *They will cleanse you of all but your sin.*
>
> *Then the baths you may try, cold and hot,*
> *If your health is not utterly spoiled,*
> *Where, whether you like it or not,*
> *They'll keep you until you are boiled.*

Then to Portland for pleasure you go,
Where the natives don't trouble a button
For you or for all that you know.
They're so proud of their stone and their mutton,

Can Weymouth be equalled? Oh no!
And here is a proof I will bring,
For besides these delights it can show
That it adds to the health of our King.

Joseph Grimaldi, the King of Clowns, was born in London on December 18 1778 – shortly before the Christmas season began – in a house among the butchers' shops of Clare Market, off Lincoln's Inn Fields. He was one of the children of an Italian, also named Joseph (or Giuseppe) Grimaldi, and his Cockney mistress, Rebecca Brooker. Both of his parents were performers themselves, at the Drury Lane Theatre. Joe's father Giuseppe was ballet-master at Drury Lane, while his mother Mrs. Brooker was a comic dancer. (It is said that Joe's father eked out his living by dentistry, and had been the official tooth-drawer to Queen Charlotte.) Joe's childhood was impoverished, and his father was a hard task master. Before he was three years old, the boy had made his first appearance in the summer theatre of Sadler's Wells, out in the Islington fields. Here Joe, accompanied by his elder sister Mary, made his debut in a pantomime called *The Wizard of the Silver Rocks: and Harlequin's Release.* Like the shows of the Commedia dell'Arte actors during their French exile, such summer performances were required to be strictly musical. Permitted shows were pantomime, ballet, comic opera, acrobatics and performing animal routines – variety acts which had come from the travelling fairs. Winter performances were allowed only at the two theatres which had been granted a royal patent. These were Drury Lane and Covent Garden.

Pantomime, that English phenomenon, has origins which are more French than Italian, coming from the Parisian theatre and the fairs. It was the usual form taken by the Commedia dell'Arte plays when they crossed the Channel. Originally, pantomime was merely an appendage to the harlequinades, in which Giuseppe Grimaldi, a noted clown, made many appearances.

By Giuseppe's time, the lovers Harlequin and Columbine had already become sideshows and a pair of buffoons, Pantaloon and Clown, held the main stage. Giuseppe played Pantaloon (his accustomed role) to great effect at Drury Lane, and in 1786 took the lesser part of Pierrot at the Haymarket Theatre. Like Baptiste Deburau later in Paris, he played Pierrot as both a cruel and melancholy figure: perhaps a portrait of himself. A haunter of graveyards in his spare time, Giuseppe was said to have been the originator of the skeleton scene, 'a dark interlude in which the Clown sometimes died of fright'. He was preoccupied with such matters: he once pretended to be dead in order to test his children's reactions to the news.

Under the strict instruction of his morbid and elderly father, Joe learned all the tricks of the trade. He knew how to tumble, performed 'skinwork' – dressed in bear or monkey skins – sang and danced. An early influence on his performance was a French artiste, Jean-Baptiste Dubois, who had previously worked in Jones's Equestrian Amphitheatre in Whitechapel, as 'clown to the horsemanship' (a role which continued in the circus). When the Amphitheatre closed down, Dubois joined the Sadler's Wells company, where he was so successful in his clowning that he appeared in the Drury Lane pantomime of 1789, *Harlequin's Frolick*. A skilled acrobat, he was famous for dancing the 'egg hornpipe' in wooden clogs. Dubois is said to have added colour to Pierrot's moony white dress, and this innovation encouraged Joe to experiment with bright shades for the clothes and make-up of his own clown.

Like Dubois, Joe was performing in character rather than comic parts when at the Wells, but at the Lane he was only appearing in crowd scenes. Then, in 1796 he appeared there as Pierrot in *Robinson Crusoe* (an adaptation which must have strayed considerably from Defoe's original novel). It was a good year for him; he met Maria, eldest daughter of Richard Hughes, who in 1791 had become the principal proprietor of the Wells, along with Weymouth and his other provincial theatres. A former actor, Hughes and his family lived in a house attached to the theatre, and it seems likely that Joe first met Maria in the dressing-room which she shared with Grimaldi's mother, Mrs. Brooker. After a long and secret engagement (Joe dared not approach Mr. Hughes for two years, until he reached his stage majority), the couple married on May 11 1799. This was perhaps the happiest time of his life.

In the Easter 1800 pantomime at the Wells, Joe played alongside Jean-Baptiste Dubois as a clown in *Peter Wilkins; or, the Flying World*. Dubois was Gobble the Eating Clown, stuffing pies and strings of sausages, while Grimaldi was Guzzle the Drinking Clown, swigging brown stage beer. (Having two clowns was a novelty; there was a pair of Harlequins as well.) Grimaldi was on his way to becoming Joey, the English clown, the forerunner of modern clowns. Joe's clown was a complex figure, with a patchwork pedigree stretching from folk fools (some of them ancient) to Shakespeare's clowns and to Clodpoll, a red-haired haired rustic and stooge, who often appeared in the pantomimes. But above all Joey was descended from the *zanni*, the clowns of the Commedia dell'Arte, from crafty, motley Harlequin – and from foolish Pierrot, with his floured face.

In 1800 he also appeared in *Harlequin Amulet; or, the Magick of Mona* at Drury Lane. In the first part he played Punch, whose hunch-back padding, mask, wooden shoes and sugar-loaf hat he claimed to find over-heavy. Later in the performance he finally came on at the Lane dressed as a Clown.

Joe's definitive success came in 1806 at Covent Garden with the pantomime *Harlequin and Mother Goose: or, The Golden Egg!* written by Thomas Dibdin. Grimaldi took the part of Squire Bugle, lord of the manor in an English village. Rural England was a new kind of setting for a pantomime story, a change from the usual Italianate scene. The whole piece, a simple one, was mimed to music, and accompanied by songs and dances. At the finale the players stepped out of their costumes, revealing their harlequinade dress underneath. Grimaldi

39 *Some of Grimaldi's clown routines, upper row and bottom row left.*

cast off his patriotic red, white and blue outfit and, wearing his clown's clothes, opened the harlequinade.

This triumphant version of *Mother Goose* ran for ninety-two nights and took over £20,000. It went on to be performed in many different countries, and one of its London performances was attended by George III, again to wide acclaim. This too was the *Mother Goose* which Deburau staged in Paris in 1830 as *Ma Mère l'Oie, ou Arlequin et L'Oeuf d'Or.*

Pantomime was gradually taking prominence over the harlequinade, with fairy-tale characters such as Cinderella, Snow White and Aladdin being used rather than Commedia figures – and Grimaldi was at the forefront of this change. With his popinjay garb, with his catch phrases of 'Hullo, Here we are again!' and 'Shall I?' (the answer undoubtedly being 'Yes!') and above all with his most famous song, 'Hot Codlins' (apples) Grimaldi was adored by his audiences:

A little old woman, her living she got
By selling codlins, hot hot hot.
And this little old woman who codlins sold
Tho' her codlins were hot, she felt herself cold.
So to keep herself warm she thought it no sin
To fetch for herself a quartern of…

When the audience supplied the missing word, Grimaldi would respond reproachfully 'Oh, for shame'. The audience joined in the chorus ('*Ri tol iddy, iddy, iddy, Ri tol iddy, iddy, Ri tol lay*') and the song continued in the same cheerful vein.

This little old woman set off in a trot,
To fetch her quartern of hot, hot, hot!
She swallowed one glass, and it was so nice,
She tipped off another in a trice;
The glass she filled till the bottle shrunk,
And this little woman she got…

And drunker still, as the song went on.

This little old woman, while muzzy she got,
Some boys stole her codlins, hot, hot, hot.
Powder under her pan put, and in it round stones:

Says the little old woman: 'These apples have bones!'
The powder the pan in her face did send,
Which sent the old woman on her latter…

Another favourite song was 'Typitywichet: or Pantomimical Paroxysms' written especially for Grimaldi, in order to 'exhibit several of his peculiarly whimsical characteristics'.

I'm not in mood for crying,
Care's a silly calf,
If to get fat you're trying,
The only way's to laugh.

Grimaldi could undoubtedly make people laugh. 'I am grim all day,' he used to quip. 'But I can make you laugh at night!' He was loved by both his London and provincial audiences.

40 *Grimaldi drawing the crowds, by George Cruikshank.*

Joe sang, and performed energetic stunts so vigorously that by the time of his retirement he had during his career broken or damaged every bone in his body. Grimaldi was famous too for his inventiveness – Phyllis Hartnoll has described how he could make 'a post-chaise out of a basket and some cheeses, or a hussar's uniform from a coal-scuttle, a pelisse, and a muff'. He played Shakespeare, too, and was an expert mime. Reading his songs now – and surviving examples of his patter – it's not easy to appreciate his humour. His direct comic heir and fellow Londoner, Dan Leno, has fared rather better, perhaps because he lived somewhat nearer to modern times, dying in 1904 at the age of forty-three. His wry monologues are still funny, like this one with Leno as the dame Widow Twankey in *Aladdin*, describing her attempts to earn a living:

> Oh dear! What is there about washing that makes people so bad-tempered? I'm sorry I ever adopted it as a profession. But there, when Mustapha left me to battle with an untrusting world what could I do? I tried lady barbering, but the customers were too attentive and I – poor simple child – was full of unsophisticatedness and I believed their honeyed words. I remember Lord Pumpler agitated me so with his badinage that there was a slight accident. I believe he would have proposed to me, but in my confusion I cut the end of his nose off. Ah! It was a close shave.

Leno's songs, such as 'Not one word said the hard-boiled egg' (of which a scratchily mournful recording survives) still seem funny too. Music Hall acts could be crude, rude or blatantly obvious, but a certain 'sophisticatedness' had also crept in. There is not, alas, any chance of hearing Grimaldi's husky voice with its woodpecker shrieking. Rough and ready though he could be, he was a gentle clown by Georgian standards, and the death in childbirth of his beloved wife Maria and her baby, only seventeen months after their wedding, must have added a strain of sadness to his performance. (Two days after her death, he was playing the Second Gravedigger in *Hamlet* at Drury Lane.)

By the time Grimaldi appeared before the King in Weymouth, he was already a popular figure. Unfortunately, his published memoirs make scant reference to the occasion. These were worked on first by journalist and playwright Thomas Egerton Wilks and later by Charles Dickens, who became involved in the editing through his great liking for clowns and for pantomime, and ultimately for Grimaldi himself. The two men were not unalike in some ways, notably in the great energy which wore them both out so that they (and Leno too) died comparatively young. Grimaldi's original, much longer (and even more inaccurate) manuscript has been lost – but Grimaldi himself is still celebrated as the greatest of all the Clowns, and the first real pantomime dame. His songs continued to be sung for years after his death. There was even a Grimaldi puppet on the London streets in Victorian times, who did 'tumbling and posturing, and a comic dance, and so forth, such as trying to catch a butterfly'.

Joe is buried at St. James's, Pentonville Hill, where his tombstone still stands in the public garden. Now, though, his name is more usually associated with the clowns' church of Holy Trinity at Dalston in East London, where he is commemorated annually. And Joey his creation, jolly, irrepressible Joey, still accompanies Mr. Punch in his shows. Joey and his swaying string of sausages are quite outside Punch's control. When Punch tries to count the bodies of his victims, the Clown will cheerfully confuse the count, interposing his own body or removing the corpse of one of the others. Punch does not retaliate: traditionally, Joey is the single puppet character whom he in all his fury does not try to kill.

Perhaps in his own way Mr. Punch too is paying his respects to the memory of the greatest of the English Clowns.

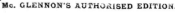

41 *Dan Leno and some of his songs.*

A Pinch of Salt

Weymouth, of late years, has been much frequented for its commodious Sea-Bathing, which it furnishes, in a manner superior to any other place in the Kingdom. The general Tranquillity of the bay, the Clearness of the Water, the Softness, and almost imperceptible descent of its Shore, are so favourable for the Purpose of Bathing, even to the most timorous and debilitated, that I do not wonder at its being the Resort of many people of the first Distinction.

Dr. John Crane, *Cursory Observations on Sea-Bathing*, c.1788

Oh, I do like to be beside the seaside,
I do like to be beside the sea…

Mark Sheridan, 1909

FROM THE VERY beginning the sea was the reason for Weymouth's existence. The old town rears up above the southern side of the harbour, above the fishing boats and ferries, and it was primarily as a port that Weymouth earned its living. There was always some fishing too. In 1829, the following fish could be bought in the fish market: '*Skate, Thornbeck, Sting Ray, Mackerel, Tunny, Red Mullet, Gurnard, Pike, Grey Mullet, Common Cod, Haddock, Whiting, Hake, Ling, Plaice, Dab, Flounder, Sole, Turbot, Common Smelt, Herring, Sprat, Lobster, Shrimp, Crab, Conger Eel, Scuttle Fish, Sunfish and Sea Horse*'. As well as variety, there was plenty. Around 1792 Peter Delamotte (father of the artist William) gave an instance of the richness of the sea's harvest in his Weymouth guide. The return of the fishing-boats could draw crowds.

This operation of hauling the Seyne (a fishing-net of prodigious length so called) is greatly attended to by strangers, when it is no uncommon thing for the fishermen to bring to shore from five to twenty or thirty thousand Herrings or Mackerel at a draught, according to their respective seasons.

Other attempts were made to capitalise on the briny, especially since the sea at Weymouth was claimed to have an 'unusual saltiness'. Over the years there were many requests for permission to collect the salt, especially from the salterns of the Town Marsh. The salterns were mudflats, reached by the tides and 'contiguous to the harbour' – and the requests were usually refused.

The area north of the harbour and along the beach was once a separate settlement. Melcombe Regis was amalgamated with its larger neighbour in the Charter of Union 1571, and from that date both places were usually referred to as Weymouth. The suffix 'Regis' refers not to George III but to Edward I, as his bride Eleanor of Castile was given Melcombe as a wedding present in 1254. In 1348 Melcombe was to have the unenviable distinction of being the port through which the Black Death entered the country.

Melcombe's most significant growth did not begin until the late eighteenth century, when people began coming to Weymouth to take the waters. The whole town was by then urgently in need of rescue. In his *New Weymouth Guide* J. Commins described how the place had been declining – it was 'fast sinking into its original insignificance' for a number of reasons. These included the removal of the wool staple to Poole, the loss of the Newfoundland trade, the ill-effects of civil war, plus 'damage by fire, neglect, want of public spirit...' Economically and socially, Weymouth was demoralised.

Three of the people who can arguably be given credit for the upturn in the borough's fortunes are Ralph Allen, James Hamilton, who was responsible for many of Weymouth's finest buildings, including the Royal Crescent – and His Majesty King George III.

Ralph Allen (1694–1764) had made his fortune in Bath. He began by reorganising the postal system there so efficiently that his method was used countrywide. His subsequent investment in the great quarries of Bath stone which surrounded the city was to make him a wealthy man. Yet he remained a kindly one, and is believed to be the model for the benevolent Squire Allworthy in Fielding's *Tom Jones*. In 1750 he bought what is now 2 Trinity Road, on the Weymouth side of the harbour, where he spent part of the summer in his 'maritime retreat'. His wife was unwell, and it was hoped that 'taking the waters' would help her recovery. Fashionable Bath, a well-established spa, was now to have a coastal outpost in Weymouth, and new-fangled ideas began to spread through the town for exploiting the sea for bathing as well for drinking the waters.

These ideas received medical backing from the resident Weymouth physician Dr. John Crane, who in his *Cursory Observations on Sea-Bathing: the use of Sea-Water Internally, and the Advantages of a Maritime Situation, as condusing to Health & Longevity* [c.1788] praised the clear pure sea water. (He also pointed out another of the resort's great and permanent advantages, remarking that 'The declivity [of the beach] is so gradual as to be almost imperceptible: a great security to the weak and fearful.')

To facilitate the water-taking, an esplanade was built. This too was not before time, as the 'parade' which preceded it had been used as a rubbish tip and was known as 'the Mixen'. The new construction was described by Delamotte in 1791 as being about half a mile long and stretching from 'Quay to Hotel'. The walk was 'beautifully bordered with turf and a grass slope of near eight feet which leads to the sands'. It occupied the space between the beach and the road in front of the houses. In 1800 the construction of a wall six feet high and two feet thick was agreed, paid for partly by subscription. Since the work began, naturally enough, opposite the King's Gloucester Lodge and the houses in Gloucester Row, one of the subscribers would have been the King himself. The work slowly continued northwards, with a line of stone posts and chains separating esplanade from road. It was impressive enough to be described in 1841 as 'one of the finest marine promenades'. The official Weymouth guide from as early as 1915 (and for many years afterwards, as the publishers unashamedly and cheerfully recycled both photographs and text) shows a dense hedge in place of the posts. The Esplanade was widened in 1922, in a scheme intended both to help the local unemployed and to prevent the shingle encroaching. This was when the Jubilee Clock, which had been erected on the sands, found itself on drier land.

By 1785, around the time the idea of an esplanade was first mooted, bathing machines were lumbering across the beach. They cost sixpence, or a shilling for one with an umbrella, and were octagonal wheeled huts, horse-drawn and unwieldy, which carried the bather into the sea, allowing him (or her) to disrobe discreetly during the journey. For an extra sixpence, a dipper awaited the bather in the sea. On arrival, the horse was unhitched, the sea-facing doors were opened

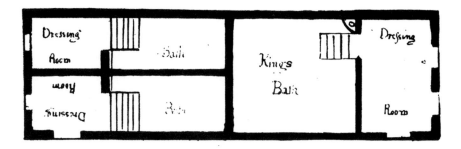

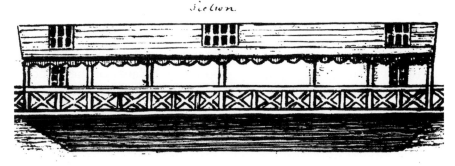

42 *The Royal Bathing Machine in its more elaborate form.*

and the bather was immersed.. The process was reversed on the return trip. A machine supposed to have been used by the King on some of his early visits, and still bearing the Royal Arms, can be seen on the Esplanade. Before its rescue it had served as a summerhouse, a common fate of the obsolete machines.

The royal connection began in about 1780 when one of George III's brothers, the Duke of Gloucester, built a house on the seafront which he named Gloucester Lodge, on the then narrow spit of land between the Backwater and the Bay. The red-brick building with its shell-like venetian windows still stands, though obscured by an unlovely veranda across its front and with a later addition of 1862, originally known as the Country Club, to its right. In George's day, the entrance was at the side, with an enclosed garden – a pleasure ground called The Shrubbery – adjoining the house. (The Gloucester Hotel, as it became, was seriously damaged by fire in 1927. Though the exterior walls remained intact, the interior had to be rebuilt.) The King first came to stay there in 1789 after recovering from his initial and probably most severe fit of madness. Formerly the most indulgent and uxorious of husbands, in his distressing insanity (now generally believed to have been porphyria, a rare hereditary disease) he had turned lewd, violent and irrational, as mad and unruly as Mr. Punch.

The gentle Weymouth world suited the convalescent King and his family, and they continued to visit Weymouth regularly – a total of fourteen times between 1789 and 1805. In 1801 George bought the house from his brother, and it became known as the Royal Lodge. The King and his family would stay all summer long – 'till the corn turns yellow', as Hardy put it in *The Trumpet-Major*. For a while, Weymouth was the summer home of the English court, and the Royal Lodge its unassuming palace. Its importance soon grew because of the French wars, as resident diarist Elizabeth Ham noted. 'The influx of visitors at such time was very great. The Continent was quite shut to the British idler, and Weymouth was all the fashion.'

This modest little world suited a King and Queen already known for their parsimony: to reduce expenses, they even brought their own food – and spring water – with them. As 'Peter Pindar' (Dr. John Wolcot) observed in 'The Royal Tour and Weymouth Amusements'

Bread, cheese, salt, catchup, vinegar, and mustard,
Small beer, and bacon, apple pye and custard;
All, all from WINDSOR greets his frugal GRACE,
For WEYMOUTH is a d-mn'd expensive place.

The unfortunate residents, however, had no choice but to pay the inflated prices which were one of the drawbacks of Weymouth's new-found prominence and prosperity. ''Tis a shilling for this, half-a-crown for that; if you only eat one egg, or even a poor windfall of an apple, you've got to pay...King George hev' ruined the town for other folks,' grumbles Uncle Benjy in *The Trumpet-Major*.

Despite such apparent privations, George III was popular in Weymouth. Over the fifty-six years of his reign, his general popularity waxed and waned, but he was always welcome in the town. The King's first seaside visit in 1789 provided weighty inspiration for local poet and printer, William Holloway, as did his third appearance in 1792 when the following ode was published:

ODE *on his* MAJESTY'S ARRIVAL *at* WEYMOUTH

O THOU! Whose fame. With undiminish'd rays,
From utmost *Indus* to the frozen Pole
Conspicuous shines, and claims the meed of praise
Where'er the wild winds blow, or waters roll;
With beating hearts thee, mighty GEORGE, we greet,
And hail thee doubly welcome to our calm retreat!

(and so on, for seven more floridly inflated stanzas).

His Majesty's first and eagerly-anticipated arrival had attracted the most attention. He was rapturously greeted by the inhabitants as he had been everywhere he passed on his journey from Windsor. His subjects rejoiced that their King was well again. Fanny Burney recorded his Weymouth welcome in a letter to her father, included in her diary.

> They have dressed out every street with labels of 'God save the King'; all the shops have it over the doors, all the children wear it in their caps – all the labourers in their hats, and all the sailors *in their voices*; for they never approach the house without shouting it aloud – nor see the King, or his shadow, without beginning to huzza, and going on to three cheers.

As if this was not overwhelming enough (and Fanny Burney found it 'excessive'), the King was also an object of devotion when sea-bathing. The bathing machines had 'God save the King' across their windows, and the attendants (Burney's 'loyal nymphs') had the words both on their bonnets and around their waists. The King's personal machine was decked with the Royal Arms. As the King descended from his machine naked into the water, a band of musicians who were hidden in the neighbouring machine burst out with the same tune. This,

43 *George III bathing at Weymouth, as described by Fanny Burney and drawn by James Gillray, 1789.*

as Thomas Hardy observes in his novel, 'was possibly in the watery circumstances tolerated rather than desired by that dripping monarch'.

By 1785, 'superb' hot and cold-water baths had been built in South Parade, overlooking the Quay 'which many timid or infirm persons prefer to falling at once into the arms of Neptune'. The baths were made of Portland stone 'improved later by marble'. It was hoped that the King would make use of this new amenity, but he did so only once, saying that the baths' water 'contained less of the marine salt than that of the beach'. When he became a regular visitor, the King was provided with his own floating bathing machine, equipped with a 'modesty hood'.

Hardy's account in his autobiography makes his own sea-bathing in the resort sound a much more pleasurable (and quieter) experience. In the summer of 1869, while he was working temporarily as an architect for Crickmay's Weymouth practice at 77 St. Thomas Street, Hardy swam early each morning 'either on the pebble beach towards Preston, or diving off from a boat'. He was a good swimmer, and found the experience invigorating after the pressures of London life. He said that he 'went back ten years in his age almost as by the touch of an enchanter's wand'. He lived for some months in 1869–70 and again in 1871 at 3 Wooperton Street, where it seems probable that he, like his character Newsome in *The Mayor of Casterbridge* could see from his bow window 'a vertical strip of blue sea'. In this small house Hardy wrote parts of his first published novel *Desperate Remedies* – and it was Crickmay who sent him to supervise the church restoration of St. Juliot, near Boscastle in Cornwall, where he had a romantic encounter with the woman who was to become his first wife. Fond of the seaside town though he was (here called Creston, but in later editions, and in later works, called Budmouth), Hardy was not very complimentary about his Weymouth dancing-partners. At a local quadrille class he found 'the young ladies of Weymouth heavier on the arm than their London sisters'. In 1869 Weymouth was still assuming a fashionable face, although the railway which was to change its character had already arrived in the town. A military band played weekly in the gardens, and a garrison was still stationed there, just as it had been in Georgian times. But few people now came to take the waters, no longer swimming in the sea for health reasons, or visiting the little spas which ringed the town.

In 1782, John Byng, Viscount Torrington, had stayed at Weymouth during his *Rides Round Britain*. It was, he said, 'the resort of the giddy and gay, where the Irish beau, the gouty peer and the genteel shop-keeper blend in folly and fine breeding'. Nevertheless, he found the place dull, and remained there (as he repeatedly stated) only to please the ladies in his party. But he was much impressed by the spa at Upwey, even composing a set of verses in praise of its waters. He explained that he felt obliged to put pen to paper in the absence of a native Weymouth bard who might undertake the task. The result was his poem 'The Charms of Upwey Spring' which began:

> *Ye poets raise*
> *Sonnets of praise*
> *In well-turn'd verses sing*
> *The sylvan shades,*
> *The rural glades*
> *Whence flows the Upwey spring...*
>
> *Each belle and beau,*
> *Promiscuous go;*
> *E'en great Batheaston's king,*
> *With pride elate,*
> *Parades in state,*
> *To Upwey's famous spring.*
>
> *It is well known*
> *York, Byng, Malone*
> *Do lovely Sally bring*
> *After her dip,*
> *To take a sip*
> *Of Upwey's noted spring...*

Along with his own dips in the sea, George III too used to 'sip' the waters – both at Upwey and at the little local spa of Nottington. He would ride over the Ridgeway to the spring at the foot of the downs at Upwey. (It's said that the goblet he drank from was afterwards used as the Ascot Gold Cup.) On some maps the well was marked as the 'Royal Spring' or, more commonly, as 'The Springs'. The Royal Arms in St. Laurence, the village church, are a gift from the grateful King.

Another, more dubious, royal figure to visit the Well was the Prince of Wales who briefly reigned as Edward VIII, until he abdicated in 1936 to marry a divorcée. The Prince called at Upwey on July 23 1923, before a game of golf on Came Down. (He had visited Thomas Hardy at Max Gate three days earlier.) The Prince, it was reported, drank from a special glass 'provided by Mr. Lovell', chairman of Upwey Parish Council, and joked with Granny Smith, who with old Mrs. Jolliffe was one of the two official dispensers of the water. Presumably, in the approved manner, he threw the dregs over his left shoulder whilst making a wish – and presented an appreciatory tip to the aged attendant.

44 *Upwey Wishing Well. The card is postmarked 1928, but the scene looks earlier.*

The spring, encircled by lumpy limestone – like the sheltered seat close by – marks the source of the River Wey, the start of its short, five mile journey to Weymouth harbour and the sea. The river rises at the foot of the steep Windbatch Hill – part of the range forming the Ridgeway, which overshadows the village. The water sinks through the chalk to surface at the Wishing Well at a considerable rate, and at a steady temperature of 10.5° C. Leaving the tearooms, the river vanishes at the mill, flowing along the narrow sunless wooded valley of Upwey, through Nottington and into Radipole Lake. The demure, arcaded seat behind the well was built (like the seafront clock) to commemorate Queen Victoria's Golden Jubilee of 1887.

By the date of the Prince of Wales's visit the spring was known by its modern name, Upwey Wishing Well. It had its own station 'Upwey Wishing Well Halte', the additional olde Englishe 'e' being an oddity of spelling affected by Great Western Railway at the time. Opened in 1905, the station was uncomfortably lodged above the hairpin bend on the road at the Ridgeway. It lasted right up to 1957. The railway had

45 *Upwey Halt(e).*

46 Sugar'em Shorey and some Wishing Well customers.

reached Weymouth in 1857 (ten years after it had got to Dorchester) and Upwey mainline station was opened in 1871. At first it was situated further north than now, over the southern Bincombe road, then it was moved to the junction of the Weymouth and Abbotsbury lines in 1886 to become Upwey Junction, where it remains, though junctionless, today. Nearby there was a third station, Upwey (Abbotsbury Branch) at the start of that ambitious little line. So for a while there were three Upwey stations – none of them actually in Upwey parish.

Under whatever name, and via whichever station, it was a stiff walk from train to Well, a fact that char-a-banc promoters were quick to notice. 'People riding by Rail Motor have to walk about one mile each way from the landing stage, and "You won't forget it"'. The first char-a-bancs were horse-drawn (including Sugar'em Shorey's six-seater brake, which plied from King's Statue to the Wishing Well. A highlight of the trip came when the vehicle was driven through the waters of River Wey). Later they were motorised: a trip to the Wishing Well continued to be a traditional and popular part of any Weymouth seaside holiday. (A further attraction was the strawberry teas.)

'Wishing Well' as the name for the spring was first used in Hawley Smart's novel of 1874 *Broken Bonds*, even though the main purpose of any excursion was still to drink the waters. Most of the novel is set on Portland, and is an exciting tale of escape from the Verne prison, but the opening scene takes place on the lofty hill above Upwey village.

> The immediate left of the hill … is clothed with a belt of wood, which runs down to a brawling shallow trout stream, deepening here and there and notably at the base of this hill, where it has been artificially dammed to a cool delicious tank, known for miles round that neighbourhood as the 'Wishing Well'.

Upwey Wishing Well remains a tourist attraction, but the spa at Nottington has fallen out of use. A visit there by the indefatigable King George III forms a scene in *The Trumpet-Major*. Lovelorn Anne Garland unexpectedly encounters the King at the spa, on her sad return homeward from Portland Bill, where she had managed to catch a glimpse of her sweetheart's ship, the *Victory*, sailing to battle. Anne stops to weep in a spot which is 'lonely and still'. Behind her is a spring with a 'stone margin round it to prevent the cattle from treading in the sides and filling it up with dirt'. The King and his physician quietly approach to examine the spring 'stooping as if to smell or taste its waters'. Seeing Anne's tears, the King asks her what is wrong, and she tells him that she has just watched her beau going off to war.

Nottington spa had been in use locally since the early eighteenth century. Its waters were sulphurous (as Hardy goes on to remark) and mildly saline. Despite the usual exaggerated claims made for them, their effects were minimal, though they would probably have helped to alleviate skin disorders and irritations of the eyes, blood and urinary passages, and they were useful for washing wounds and sores. The spring was also of service in curing scabby or mangy animals – which explains the state of it when visited by Dorset historian John Hutchins. He gives a pungently immediate description of the spa in the first edition of his *History of Dorset*, 1774.

In this vill is a medicinal spring. The mud and earth about it is blue. In frosty weather it is thick and blackish, and the surface covered with a thick oily film, and never freezes. It has a strong foetid sulphureous smell, not much unlike gunpowder newly inflamed, and a flavour resembling boiled eggs, some-time rotten eggs; its colour, when viewed from above in a tin vessel, is bluish.

A 'collar' was shortly afterwards built round the spring to keep the animals away, but it was reported that diseased beasts continued to be washed in the waters. And it still had no roof. By 1790, the well was surrounded by a high circular wall, with a stone slab seat provided – but it remained open to the sky.

Despite the discomforts, the well began to attract more visitors. Dr. Pickford's *Treatise on the Quality and Virtues of Nottington Water, near Weymouth*, published around 1822, received 665 orders, mainly from eminent personages, some of them from as far away as Bath, London and even Lisbon. Drinking spa waters was regarded as an important complement to sea bathing. For ease of application, the water was often bottled and taken away, as is done by the King and his physician in *The Trumpet-Major*. The owners of the well seem to have regarded any serious commercialisation as ungentlemanly, and made no attempt to capitalise on its royal patronage. In 1829, Ellis's *History* commented: 'It is rather extraordinary that although the spring has been long known to the public, the accommodation for those who have occasion to drink it, should have been upon so limited a scale.'

Then in 1830, as a result of nearby excavations the spring resurfaced in a different place, over which was erected 'an elegant Octagon Building'. It survives today, looking charming but frail, like a lost bathing machine. Soon the building was fitted out with under-ground baths, a ground floor pump room and accommodation above. This belated exploitation of a known resource came about not only because of a change of owner, but at a time when, without royal patronage, Weymouth's fortunes were on the wane. Weymouth was still fashionable enough in 1816 to be the scene of the secret engagement of Frank Churchill and Jane Fairfax in Jane Austen's *Emma*. The turning-point was to come a year later when the Duke and Duchess of Gloucester left the town after the death of Princess Charlotte, heir to the throne and George III's only legitimate grand-child. It had been hoped that she too would make Weymouth her summer residence, but this was not to be. The Royal properties were finally sold when the King himself died in 1820. His son George IV had always much preferred Brighton where he built his own stately pleasure dome: the Pavilion.

Hawley Smart describes the smaller town's dilemma in *Broken Bonds*:

> The poor little watering-place, with one of the most beautiful bays in England, still lies paralysed under the ponderous memories of George the Third. He is like an incubus on the town. They cannot divest themselves of those heavy reminiscences. He permeates the whole neighbourhood, even to defacing an entire down with his gigantic effigy cut out on the soft green turf. You can't escape from that old Conservative monarch; you are always tumbling upon his statue, his house, his hotel, or something of that sort. Despite all his descendants have tried to do for Weymouth, Weymouth still remains enveloped in the mantle of George the Third.

At the time of its rejuvenation, Nottington Spa also acquired a rival. To announce its advent, the *Dorset County Chronicle* reprinted a prophetic poem on the subject.

> *When Dorsetshire has two Mineral Springs*
> *The Demon Disease shall take to his wings*
> *And the folk of both country and town*
> *To drink then shall come down,*

And everyone shall say
That his sickness has past away,
And the Church-yard no more shall be fed
For there'll be neither sick nor dead.

The second spa opened a year later in 1831 at Radipole. The waters had properties similar to those of Nottington, though with higher levels of hydrogen sulphide. (Of the three, only Upwey's water is pleasant to the taste.) The building, a Moorish confection, was far more fanciful than Nottington's. Well-placed, on the rise above Weymouth, it had wonderful views of town, sea and country. The well itself was set in flowery gardens which ran down to the shoreline, with pump-room and baths in separate areas. Benson's *New Weymouth Guide* of 1831 sings the praises of the new spa.

'The view is picturesque, particularly at the flow of the tide above the town, which forms a handsome lake, and throws pleasing softness on the surrounding scenery.' On this 'handsome lake' it was then possible to approach Radipole by pleasure boat, to take tea or water – though only on the spring tides, when the water could reach as high as Radipole Church.

Attractive as it certainly sounds, Radipole Spa did not last long, probably because it had begun too late. The spas at both Nottington and Radipole rapidly declined in the 1840s. A.B.Granville, a specialist on the subject, whose book was published in 1841, remarked that neither 'before or during' his visit to Weymouth did he discover the existence of either spa. Both were to become laundries: Radipole a large one, and Nottington a hand one in use before 1876. There is no trace of Radipole's spa today. It has vanished under St. Aldhelm's church and a prosaic block of flats. The names of Spa Road and of the Spa public house are the only reminders of its existence.

Among the breezy accounts of the health-giving waters of spa and sea there is recorded one local tragedy. It happened to the family of John Meade Falkner.

Falkner was a son of the senior curate of St. Mary's Church, Weymouth. The family lived in the rectory (now a café/bar) at 82 St. Thomas Street. In the smarter 'sister-house' next door lived Hardy's Weymouth employer, George Rackstraw Crickmay, 'a cheery man with much geniality and a large family of sons and daughters'. The grand double entrance to the two houses is there today. The Falkners did not use the house's dining-room 'which looked out streetwards over the stone-flagged pathway and the flights of steps and the iron railings and the great bush of St. John's wort and the worm-casted and earthy-grass cat-walk'. Instead, they used the back room, a warm, bright room which looked out over the family's fig tree and across other gardens to the Backwater. In this room on March 2 1871 their lives were changed forever. Falkner precisely recalled the events of the day some fifty years later.

> We were dining one day about 1.30 (I think that it was Thursday March 2nd 1871) and there was on the table a glass water-bottle cylindrical in shape with a flat under-side. Someone noticed that there was something, like a piece of thick black string, coiled round the bottom inside, and it was fished out. It was fished out with one of our good old silver forks, and proved to be the tail which had dropped off a decomposed rat. The Weymouth water is some of the best in the country, and comes out of the service-pipes cold clear and sparkling. But in the passage … there was the 'butler's pantry' with the usual accessories. This was fitted with a tap of soft-water supplied from a rain-water cistern and used for washing purposes because the town water was 'hard'. I believe but am not sure that servants had been specially warned that this tap was not to be used for drinking.

The rat was a typhoid rat. Of all the family of seven only John's father entirely escaped the disease, and his mother died of it. This terrible accident was to shadow the rest of John Meade Falkner's life.

48 *John Meade Falkner on the Backwater.*

Typhoid was not uncommon in Weymouth in the nineteenth century. Nor, even more dangerously, was cholera (both were water-borne diseases, though this was not realised). There was a severe cholera outbreak in the early 1830s and another more widespread epidemic, fifteen years later. In 1858–59 there were fifty-nine deaths in Weymouth from cholera.

Mortality rates in Weymouth were significantly higher than those in Melcombe Regis where the Falkners had lived, and the water supply – or lack of it – was one of the main causes. Poor sanitation was another, though this wasn't much better to the north of the town. Weymouth was once again a filthy place, with the sea its sewer.

Drinking-water on the harbour side of the Borough was supplied by two pumps, one at the end of the High Street (now to be seen outside the New Rooms Inn) and the second in 1854 by Springfield, the home of the Devenish family in Rodwell. For the use of the poor, two taps were provided on Town Bridge. Otherwise people had to resort to private springs or wells, or take water from the little River Wey.

It was different in Melcombe Regis. In 1797 the Weymouth Waterworks Act had been passed 'an Act for Supplying the Borough and Town of Weymouth and Melcombe Regis, and the parts adjacent, in the County of Dorset, with Water.' (One of the signatories was James Hamilton, Builder.) The source of the water was Boiling Rock, a spring which can still be seen in a garden above the steep and rocky road beside Chalbury Hill. ('Boiling' is here a description of the furious energetic force of the water, rather than its temperature.) The water was channelled, by gravity, through wooden pipes which were laid across Lodmoor, following the contours of the higher land to the north of the marsh and dropping down into Melcombe Regis,

Which was where the supply stopped. It was apparently not possible to take the pipes across the Harbour. But it was also true that Melcombe Regis was where the rich and influential citizenry tended to live, and where the increasing numbers of visitors stayed. The harbour-dwellers were left to fend for themselves.

The pipes were made of hollowed-out elm trunks, elm being a wood which can endure under water, and which is traditionally used for such purposes. Great chunks of elm, once buried under Lodmoor, can now be seen in Sutton Poyntz Water Museum. The rough and flaking bark shows signs of woodworm, but not of wear.

On reaching its destination, the water was fed into rather elegant clay pipes, made by R. Spencer of Sturminster Newton. These clay mains terminated in 'leaden branches' from which Melcombe Regis received its water. This supply was available from about 1810. By 1854, Boiling Rock could no longer provide for all the needs of the growing town.

On July 15 1855 an Act of Parliament was passed authorising Weymouth Waterworks Company to acquire springs at the foot of the Ridgeway above Sutton Poyntz, quite close to the White Horse Hill. (As early as 1593 the Mayor of Weymouth, Mr. T. Bareffoote, had made enquiries from the landowner about using Sutton Poyntz water, but nothing came of this approach.) The Company brought in Thomas Hawksley, eminent Victorian water engineer, who acted as consultant to the waterworks from 1854 until his death in 1893. In fact, nothing was too good for the new works. The funnel of Brunel's *Great Eastern*, blown out of the deck in an explosion on its way past Weymouth, was put into the new works as a strainer, where it stayed until 2003. And John Coode, director of the Company (and principal engineer for the building of the Breakwater in Portland Harbour) hired the well-regarded John Towlerton Leather as the main contractor. Leather built the still-existing Turbine House and an impounding reservoir, which held the water from the Spring Head. The water was pumped into Preston Reservoir on Rimbury Hill, from where it gravitated across the Harbour – and into Weymouth. To this day, Weymouth's water supply comes from Sutton Poyntz springs, but once again has had to be supplemented: this time from a borehole source at West Knighton, east of Dorchester.

Finally, it might be added that another person involved in the scheme was George Rackstraw Crickmay, Engineering Manager of the Waterworks from 1856 to 1907, sometime employer of Thomas Hardy – and next door neighbour to John Meade Falkner.

Near the top of the Esplanade is a gaily-painted statue of George III, a tribute to the king who made Weymouth famous. He stands stockily on a plinth of Portland stone, accompanied by the Lion and the Unicorn – the Royal Arms which adorn many a seaside puppet booth. Both King and royal beasts are made of a further, tougher material: Coade stone.

By the time the statue was erected in 1809, the King had ceased to visit his summer home. He had, however, been consulted about the design, and seems to have contributed towards the cost of the construction (as well as giving £200 'for the purpose of continuing the Esplanade') in 1802. He approved of the design, which showed him wearing his coronation robes. They were, he said, 'the most proper dress for the occasion'. The architect was James Hamilton, and the statue was completed by 1804, although it was not unveiled until 1810. An invoice of October 18th from Coade & Seaby, Lambeth, states that it had been safely placed on a steamer en route for Weymouth. The invoice also provides a full description of the monument:

47 King's Statue.

Modelling Statue of His Majesty in his royal robes decorated with the Order of the Garter – an antique Table supported with Lyons legs behind him bearing the Crown on his right and Books of the Constitution of England on his left – Against the Table is a very bold Cornucopia with the Arms of Great Britain and Ireland. In his Majesty's right hand, the Sceptre, at his left the Sword, Whole Extent about 14 feet by f9.i3 high. Agreed 18 Jany 1803 for 200 Guineas including the Lyon and Unicorn.

(The invoice goes on to include the company's expenses for erecting a stage during the summer months on which to display the statue.)

Great pains were taken over the inscription – of which several drafts survive – and prayers were composed for the stone-laying ceremony:

May the bountiful Hand of Heaven supply this Town with abundance of Corn, Wine Oil and all the other Conveniences of this Life.

And, after laying the stone:

As we have now laid this foundation Stone may the grand Architect of the Universe of his kind Providence enable us to carry on and finish the work which we have now begun –
May he still be the Protector of our most gracious Sovereign – whose statue we are about to erect and may he preserve it from Decay and Ruin to the latest Posterity.

This last prayer must have been answered. In place for two hundred years (and painted in suitably seaside colours since 1949 and repainted in 2008) the King's Statue, with the accompanyingly brazen Lion and Unicorn, shows few traces of wear, despite its exposed position beside the waters. Like the memories of past glory, the image of King George has survived.

It survives too in the hill figure on the downs above Osmington, a majestic sight never seen by the King, who was unfortunately blind as well as absent by the time the figure was completed. The chalk man on his white horse, 280 feet long and 320 high, and so vast that he can clearly be seen from out at sea – is a carving of George III riding with cocked hat and what Frederick Treves described as 'unreasonable' spurs. The King is riding, oddly enough, away from his favourite watering place. The design is taken from a famous portrait of the King, which has been turned nose to tail. This is doubly odd, as there is only one other equine figure, the White Horse of Uffington, which faces to the right. The horse is in the traditional shape for a hill figure, though this is the single known example with a rider, who – so the story irresistibly goes – may have been added to cover the traces of an earlier, ghostly horse.

The figure was carved on behalf of the grateful citizens of Weymouth in 1808, three years after the King's last visit to the town.

49   White Horse, Osmington, as it is today.

Since this was a private initiative, unlike the statue, there are no records of the horse's creation. The date had been a matter of contention until the publication of an article by Maureen Boddy and Jack West in the *Dorset Yearbook*, 1985. They discovered a reference to the precise time – May to August 1808 – which was noted by Thomas Oldfield Bartlett in his journal. The *Sherborne Mercury* of October 10 1808, also provides a description of the 'equestrian figure of his Majesty on his favourite grey charger'. It's known that the designer was the versatile James Hamilton, architect of Georgian Weymouth. Hamilton directed twelve army engineers in the drawing of the outline. Horse and rider stride majestically across land then owned by John Wood, a Weymouth bookseller, while the bill was paid by John Rainier.

The outline of the horse may have been cut by the soldiers and military engineers who were encamped around the downs. In *The Trumpet-Major*, John Loveday points out to Anne Garland the distant 'scratches of white' now showing on the green hillside. 'The King's head is to be as big as our mill-pond' he explains, 'and his body as big as this garden; he and the horse will cover more than an acre.' Loveday and Anne Garland make a special outing to see it. 'When they reached the hill they found forty navvies at work removing the dark sod so as to lay bare the chalk beneath.' Viewed so closely, the figure is 'scarcely intelligible'. This fictional visit, somewhat earlier than was possible, probably added to the confusion over the dating of the figure's creation. Despite his research, and the careful accuracy of the historical scenes, Hardy was somewhat vague about the exact chronological placing of purely fictional scenes.

In 1880, when *The Trumpet-Major* was published, the white horse must have looked rather different from how it looks today. When described by Frederick Treves in *Highways and Byways in Dorset* (1906) and foggily illustrated in grey and white by Joseph Pennell, the monarch was said to be 'less imposing than the animal'. The problem was – and is – that the figure has to be regularly scraped. According to the account of local journalist Jarvis Harker in *Sketches Written In, Round, and About Weymouth* [1877] the practice had faltered. 'For some fifty years, one James Hardy took pride and delight grooming steed and man, but he was gathered to his fathers some seven years ago.' Now steed and man were neglected.

> *The owld White Harse wants zetting to rights,*
> *If some un ull promise good cheer,*
> *They'll gee un a scrape to kip un in zhape,*
> *And a'll last for many a year.*

The horse's grooming over the years continued to be a hit-and-miss affair. No attempt was made to camouflage this, the largest of the hill figures, during the Second World War, but weeds and grass provided a natural obscurity. In the photograph which appears in *White Horses and Other Hill Figures* (1949), the King is an etiolated, beaky figure on a stout-bellied, trotting horse. Details of his hands and of his mount's reins are carefully outlined.

The horse today, with its rider squarely mounted, is more streamlined and confident, though its tail continues to look 'like a chalk road descending the hill' as it did when Treves visited around 1906. The carving is skilfully done, and has none of the flat and elongated appearance of others from its stable. Hamilton has made allowances for the slope and for the low viewpoint. Silently, as ghostly as the old horse beneath the dark earth, George III still rides the glossy downlands, above the town he made his own.

50 White Horse sketched in 1949.

Water, Water, Everywhere

Oh, the grand old Duke of York
He had ten thousand men.
He marched them up to the top of the hill
And he marched them down again.
And when they were up they were up,
And when they were down they were down,
And when they were only half way up
They were neither up nor down.

Nursery rhyme, said to describe Prince Frederick's drilling of his
troops on Bincombe Hill, Weymouth

51 Vignette by Thomas Hardy for 'The Alarm' in Wessex Poems, 1898

I F WATER BROUGHT WEALTH and health to Weymouth, it also
served another vital function, by protecting the town and its hinter-
land from invasion. The Channel at Weymouth is quite narrow, due to
the outreach of Portland from the English coast, and of the Cap de la
Hague from the French side. But the sea proved to be wide enough in
the early years of the nineteenth century to keep Napoleon and his
army out of a town which had considerable contemporary strategic
importance as the site of the King's summer court.

Thomas Hardy was born in Dorset in 1840, and when he was a child the Napoleonic Wars (1799–1815) were still well within living memory. The name of Napoleon Bonaparte could yet raise a shiver of fear. Hardy's paternal grandfather had been a volunteer, and his story is told in 'The Alarm', in *Wessex Poems* (1898). A drawing by the author shows his father's father ('a harnessed Volunteer') marching, lonely and upright, over the winding Ridgeway road to join the Yeomanry at Weymouth in 1803. To his relief (his wife is expecting a child and he does not want to leave her) the alarm is a false one, like others of that troubled time.

It was easy enough to panic, especially in 1804 when Napoleon's forces were assembled at Boulogne. On a clear day it was possible to see the glitter of their weapons on the far side of the Channel. In *The Trumpet-Major* (in a chapter also called 'The Alarm') the narrator remarks how 'At the distance of Boulogne details were lost, but we were impressed on fine days by the novel sight of a huge army moving and twinkling like a school of mackerel under the rays of the sun.' Weymouth was eager to respond. Beacons were ready on the surrounding hilltops, and the Downs were alive with soldiers. The town possessed three barracks: Red Barracks on the Nothe, Queen's Barracks at

52 *Drawing by Hardy for 'The Alarm' in Wessex Poems.*

Coneygar Lane and the largest group of buildings at Radipole, on Lodmoor Hill. Warships, too, lay waiting in the Bay.

Not all the soldiers were local. Among the men camped out on the downs were soldiers from the King's home country, described by Hardy in his short story 'The Melancholy Hussar of the German Legion', written in 1889.

> Here stretch the downs; high and breezy and green, absolutely unchanged since those eventful days. A plough has never disturbed the turf, and the sod that was uppermost then is uppermost now. Here stood the camp; here are distinct traces of the banks thrown up for the horses of the cavalry, and spots where the midden-heaps lay are still to be observed. At night, when I walk across the lonely place, it is impossible to avoid hearing, amid the scourings of the wind over the grass-bents and thistles, the old trumpet and bugle calls, the rattle of the halters; to help seeing rows of spectral tents and the *impedimenta* of the soldiery. From within the canvases come guttural syllables of foreign tongues, and broken songs of the fatherland; for they were mainly regiments of the King's German Legion that slept round the tent-poles hereabouts at that time.

The Melancholy Hussar, Matthäus Tina, is one of the York Hussars, much fêted in Weymouth for their magnificent uniforms, their fine horses and (according to Hardy) their moustaches, rarely seen in the country before. Equally exotic was the Waltz, the dance the Hussars brought with them from Germany. Elizabeth Ham wrote that 'This was the first we had ever seen of this kind of dance, now so common. Nothing but Country Dances were then in vogue.'

Matthäus falls in love with Phyllis, a local girl, and they plan to flee England together by boat. Their plan goes astray; Matthäus and his fellow-deserter and friend, Christoph, are caught and sentenced to death by firing-squad. Their deaths are witnessed from the lovers' trysting-place by the unsuspecting Phyllis.

This quiet tragedy, set under the Ridgeway in Bincombe, is rooted in the truth. The village's parish registers record the burial of a pair of Hussars 'Shot for Desertion' in 1801. Death could be found even amongst the colour, movement and excitement of the encampments before battle had even begun.

For German or Briton, soldier, sailor or civilian, danger was ever-present and rumours of invasion were rife. On a foggy day in May 1804, word went round that Napoleon had actually landed on or near Portland. Some island fishermen reported that they had become lost in the fog off the coast and found themselves in the middle of a fleet of warships. Although this turned out to be yet another false alarm, the possibility of invasion remained, a possibility realised by one of the spectators watching the King reviewing his troops on the downs in *The Dynasts*: 'Gloucester Lodge could be surrounded, and George and Queen Charlotte carried off before he could put on his hat, or she her red coat and pattens!' The possibility always remained in Hardy's imaginings. In a short story called 'A Tradition of Eighteen Hundred and Four', Hardy tells of a shepherd boy who encountered

Bonaparte one night on the hills above Lulworth Cove. Sadly, there's no evidence of such an event, but Hardy is dreamily evoking a half-myth, half-belief of those frightening days.

The Trumpet-Major takes place entirely in and around an embattled Weymouth, with the garrisoned soldiers waiting for something to

53 Napoleon, from a volume belonging to Thomas Hardy.

54 Jug, with caricature of Napoleon, belonging to Thomas Hardy.

happen, or reporting on distant battles they have endured. Hardy's other work on these times, which was conceived before the novel but did not appear in full until 1908, was his epic-drama *The Dynasts*, which takes a broader, bolder, much more ambitious approach, with scenes which range all over war-torn Europe. One magnificent chorus on the Eve of Waterloo has a quick sympathy with the suffering of animals trapped by the fighting.

Several scenes from *The Dynasts* are set in what Hardy calls 'South Wessex' and show the homelier experiences of the Dorset people during the French Wars. Watching 'King Garge' review his troops above Weymouth (a regular duty) another of the spectators remarks sagely:

> *And what a time we do live in,*
> *between wars and wassailings, the goblin o' Boney,*
> *and King George in flesh and blood!*

'Boney' was Napoleon Bonaparte: the goblin, the bogeyman, and the subject of much cheerful, cheeky caricature in England. In *The Trumpet-Major* the narrator remarks on how 'The religion of the country had, in fact, changed from love of God to hatred of Napoleon Buonaparte...' and later describes how 'we punned on Buonaparte and his gunboats, chalked his effigy on stage-coaches, and published the same in prints.' He had become a national obsession.

Napoleon's gloomy, charismatic features appeared on china mugs and jugs, in cartoons and in hieroglyphs. Hieroglyphic portraits of

Bonaparte, often difficult to decipher, were very popular at the time. A typical example – not unlike the one the writer himself owned – is described in *The Trumpet-Major*. 'The hat represented a maimed French eagle; the face was ingeniously made up of human carcases, knotted and writhing together in such directions as to form a physiognomy; a band, or stock, shaped to resemble the English Channel, encircled his throat, and seemed to choke him; his epaulette was a hand tearing a cobweb that represented the treaty of peace with England; his ear was a woman crouching over a dying child.'

With the possible exception of Hitler, no English adversary has been so thoroughly lampooned. Napoleon was used as the devil-figure in Punch & Judy, and in mummers' plays he was given the role previously taken by the villainous Turkish Knight, with George III in the part more often played by old St. George. He is there in the local Lulworth play, *The Battle of Waterloo*, performed on Christmas Eve every year until 1914. Bonaparte was the folk-enemy *par excellence*.

Hardy was fascinated by Napoleon, though this is not a reason he gave for writing *The Dynasts*. He claims in his preface that the choice of such a subject came because 'the writer was familiar with a part of England that lay within hail of the watering-place in which King George the Third had his favourite summer residence during the war with the first Napoleon and where he was visited by ministers and others who bore the weight of English affairs on their more or less competent shoulders at that stressful time.' Yet only two scenes of *The Dynasts* are set in Weymouth town. The first takes place at the King's home in Gloucester Lodge, where the monarch is urgently conferring with his Prime Minister, William Pitt the Younger. In the midst of grave danger the King still finds time to put in a good word for his favourite watering-place.

> *Your visit to this shore is apt and timely,*
> *And if it do but yield you needful rest*
> *From fierce debate, and other strains of office*
> *Which you and I in common have to bear,*

'Twill be well earned. The bathing is unmatched
Elsewhere in Europe, – see its mark on me! –
The air like liquid life…

The King seems in life to have been as unflappable as he sounds in this passage from the drama. His ministers had been worried at the prospect of his summer removals to Weymouth, and by his insouciant habit of paying unannounced calls on his subjects in the surrounding countryside – Farmer George liked to discuss agriculture with the natives. Chief magistrate Richard Ford was assigned to his protection, along with a squad of Bow Street constables. Although he could be over-zealous at times, Ford had real reason for alarm during a performance at the town's theatre on August 31 1801 attended by the King and his family. The constables had become suspicious of a drunkard who was sitting in the audience, but trouble actually came when a London lace and garter hawker called Urban Metcalf tried to jump into the Royal Box, but was restrained by one of the Bow Street men. Later a penknife was found embedded in the stage door beside the box. Metcalf was detained, but escaped from his lock-up and created a disturbance outside the Royal Lodge. He was incarcerated in Bedlam, as it was decided that anyone who attempted to kill by hurling a penknife from such a distance must surely be mad, and security around the monarch was tightened. The King's entourage were troubled by his frequent proximity to his subjects when in Weymouth, but the King remained unalarmed, as he did in the face of more serious attempts on his life – though the Queen and the six princesses were 'seriously frightened'.

George took this, as he took other personal assaults, in his stride. He was accustomed to these and wider dangers. The French Revolution had broken out shortly before his first stay in Weymouth – the storming of the Bastille took place the day before his first visit to the Weymouth theatre, and the events across the water remained always in the background, inevitably affecting the atmosphere of his visits. A guard ship accompanied the Royal party whenever they sailed in the Bay – a favourite occupation of the King's. At least twice a carriage was made ready and drawn up in front of the Royal Lodge in case there was a need for a swift escape for the family.

Not all the news was bad. On October 2 1798 a horseman galloped into Weymouth. He had ridden from London in nine hours and fifteen minutes, and carried a personal letter from Admiral Nelson to King George, announcing England's defeat of the French at the Battle of the Nile, one month previously. A ball at Stacie's Hotel was interrupted by the report of Nelson's victory which was received with great rejoicing, and the evening performance at the Theatre Royal was also interrupted for an announcement of this crucial news.

The following night, the Royal Family themselves went to the theatre. The celebrations must surely have outshone the performance, if an unknown eye witness is to be believed.

> As soon as the curtain was drawn up, Mr. Fisher [a member of the cast] came forward and spoke an occasional address on Admiral Nelson's Victory, which was received with the most rapturous applause: and *God Save the King* was sung, the whole house joining in full chorus. After the play, the manager, Hughes, displayed a beautiful transparency of the figures of Britannia, treading Anarchy and Rebellion under her feet, which had a very striking effect.

The Royal Family, their entourage and even the comedians were garlanded with oak and laurel, and outside in the Bay fireworks lit the water.

The story goes that Mr. Punch was too involved in these events:

> After the battle of the Nile, Lord Nelson figured on one of the street-stages, and held a dialogue with Punch, in which he endeavoured to persuade him, as a brave fellow, to go on board his ship, and assist in fighting the French: 'Come, Punch, my boy, (said the naval hero,) I'll make you a captain or commodore, if you like it.' – 'But I don't like it, (replied the puppet-show hero;)

I shall be drowned.' – 'Never fear that, (answered Nelson;) he that is born to be hanged, you know, is sure not to be drowned.'

On the next day the King, while yet in Weymouth, promptly created Admiral Nelson a peer of the realm. He had become considerably less enthusiastic about his new peer by the time of Nelson's greatest victory at the Battle of Trafalgar (1805) in which the Admiral lost his life. Despite this sacrifice and the importance of the victory, Nelson was latterly disliked by the King, who strongly disapproved of his adulterous relationship with Emma Hamilton.

Thomas Hardy was particularly interested in another of the war's heroes, with whom he liked to claim kindred. He was Thomas Masterman Hardy, born at nearby Portesham, 'the snug village under Blackdon hill', where his house still stands, overlooked by a sturdy stone lion. Hardy gave this hero's proximity as his third major reason for writing *The Dynasts*. Thomas Masterman was the same Hardy who was present at Nelson's death on board the *Victory*.

The Battle of Trafalgar and its consequences are discussed in the drama by the drinkers in the Old Rooms Inn, during *The Dynasts'* second Weymouth scene. The men claim that Nelson's body was brought home in a 'case of sperrits' – spirits drunk dry by the crew on the long journey home. Thus cheered, they sing together the hearty 'new ballet' about Nelson's victory:

In the wild October night-time, when the wind raved round the land,
And the Back-sea met the Front-sea, and our doors were blocked with
    sand,
And we heard the drub of Dead-man's Bay, where bones of thousands are,
We knew not what the day had done for us at Trafalgar.
    Had done,
    Had done,
    For us at Trafalgar!

From 'Song, The Night of Trafalgar'

The 'front sea' crossed the Esplanade to meet the Backwater on many a wild night. In his memoir, John Meade Falkner remarked that living, as his aunts did, in Brunswick Terrace, was like living 'on board ship'. Until the Breakwater was built, 'there were always iron shutters kept in readiness to fix in the ground-floor windows, to withstand the shower of pebbles which a wild south-western gale flung up'. Brown paper was stuffed into cracks and sandbags placed in the centre of the frames. The building of the Breakwater, which reduced the number of shipwrecks around the island of Portland, also brought greater tranquillity to the Bay. The foundation stone was laid by Prince Albert, who was much interested in the venture, in 1849. The immensely ambitious building works became Dorset's number one tourist attraction. Convict labour was used for digging out the stone and the prisoners were housed in the purpose-built Grove – which also attracted visitors. Eventually postcards could be bought bearing the legend 'Just Arrived Here' and showing an unhappy line of newly-transported convicts. As well as poaching some of Weymouth's trade, the undertaking probably contributed to the southbound shift of pebbles across the beach.

Falkner remembered that when the sea swept over the Narrows to join the Backwater, stepping-stones were laid 'for the commodity of passengers'. This too was not unusual. The Narrows was the spit of land reaching from Gloucester Lodge down towards Greenhill, between the sea and the Backwater. A painting by King George's protégé, William Delamotte, shows a view of the Narrows from along the turnpike to the lonely Lodge, which stands like a stage set in the distance. Block by block, the strip became filled with hotels and terraces of houses. The land behind it was drained after 1830 for a park, a project which was never realised. Weymouth's history is one of slow reclamation of land from the waters: the Town Marsh was infilled, the Backwater and Lodmoor tamed, and the Harbour narrowed. But the battle with the unpredictable sea goes on, and storms can still cause serious damage.

Of all the storms, the one never to be forgotten was the Great Gale of November 1824 when the entire Esplanade was destroyed overnight. This momentous event was breathlessly described in Ellis's *History Of Weymouth and Melcombe Regis* (1829), either by an eye witness to the occasion, or with vivid hindsight.

> Tuesday, November 23rd, 1824, the sun arose, and exhibited to the inhabitants, Weymouth nearly destroyed, by the tempestuous ravages of a raging insetting sea; vast rolling surges rushed furiously onwards, – and billows, gigantic in their rage, frowned horribly; which, with the terrific roar of the tempest, – the shrill yells of the seabirds, – the look of unutterable anguish, – the piteous moan of the ingulphed mariner, – the horrid crash of nature's warfare, – and death, in all its tremendous majesty, – combined to render a scene, at all times grand – now, sublimely aweful.

The edge of the Esplanade was marked by a series of stone blocks, linked by heavy chains. The waves tossed away chains and blocks 'as

55 Painting by William Delamotte of the approach to Weymouth from the north.

if they were rubble'. Not many remain; there are ten, square and sturdy, opposite the Pier Bandstand, while another is set in the wall of a raised flowerbed on the Esplanade opposite the Dorothy Inn. Although now almost indecipherable, this bears the words 'Esplanade Destroyed by a Tempest Novr 23rd 1824'. Further memorials to the 'Tempest' can be found along the Dorset coast and inland as far as Dorchester. The old church at Fleet, which features in the opening chapters of John Meade Falkner's most famous novel *Moonfleet*, was left with only its chancel intact and a new church was built further inland to replace it. In Weymouth, the Esplanade's stone blocks and chains were also replaced, and Falkner remembered them in the 1860s. He said they had a nautical appearance. (There were a few seats, too – 'nice old large straight-backed wooden ones, painted green'.)

The Falkner family home, the Old Rectory in St. Thomas Street, did not escape watery invasion, seeming to be especially vulnerable to it. Sometimes rainwater would pour like a torrent through the roof to form a cascade 'over the broad steps of the gloomy well-stair-case', a defect which the Rector, out of harm's way on higher ground, refused to remedy on the grounds of economy. The deluge happened so frequently that the family eventually took it for granted: the 'rain-blotched walls and stair-cataracts, were accepted as heaven-sent dispensations and referred to in the family as "common objects of the sea-shore"'.

Worse still was the damage from the sea:

> While rain-floods were attacking the upper parts of the house, sea-floods were attacking the lower. The drainage of Weymouth was generally very defective or non-existent; and the drainage of the Old Rectory was particularly bad. At certain Spring Tides and with certain strong winds, the water in that saltwater estuary at the back of the house was backed up till there was a flood in the 'Backwater'. At such times the drains of the house ceased to act, and the sea-water was forced

up them with such pressure as to break up sinks and other effluents, and flood the basement with a filthy and noisesome inundation.

Seawater in the cellar, rain on the roof – the sea had turned invader, and it's little wonder that in 1881 the family finally moved away. The Revd Charles Falkner became Curate-in-Charge of the wooded hamlet of Buckland Ripers, a few miles out of Weymouth, and a very different world. The nearest coastal village was Fleet, behind the Chesil Bank, where much of *Moonfleet* (1898) takes place.

Moonfleet begins and ends with wild November seas breaking over the Chesil, in great gales like that of 1824. Although the story tells of the dramatic changes these two storms make to the life of the hero and narrator, John Trenchard, the dominant character in the novel is always the sea.

56 *Punch and Judy at the Seaside'.*
Drawing by Robert Barnes, showing Professor Murray's booth.

Mr. Punch

A DRAWING BY ROBERT BARNES called 'Punch & Judy at the Seaside' shows a performance on a bustling beach at Weymouth. The puppeteer was Professor Murray of Bristol.

Little is known about either painter or Punch & Judy man. Robert Barnes was a genre painter and illustrator who worked on various publications including the *Graphic*, where in 1885 he produced twenty illustrations for the serial issue of Hardy's novel, *The Mayor of Casterbridge*, published in 1886. Despite his name, Barnes was not a local man. He was born in 1840 (the same year as Hardy) lived in Great Berkhampstead, Redhill and latterly, Brighton. He visited Dorchester in 1885 to see for himself the author and the places mentioned in the novel: Grey's Bridge and Maumbury Rings, for example, both appear in his illustrations. Whilst in the county, he must have visited Weymouth, and sketched the Punch & Judy show in action. His drawings for *The Mayor of Casterbridge*, some of the better illustrations for a Hardy novel, are at their best when depicting crowded scenes – the furmity woman and her customers at the fair, or the smoky, boozy interior of the King of Prussia tavern are far livelier than his other over-stylised set pieces involving two or three characters.

Barnes's Weymouth scene is no exception to this rule-of-thumb. A crowd has gathered in front of the booth – which is Professor Murray's own, with his elaborate decorated proscenium and multi-striped cloth. The audience is gossipy, restless, unruly. Adults gather on the Esplanade hoping no doubt, in immemorable fashion, to avoid paying for their entertainment. Behind them, the skyline and the rounded end of St. Mary Street are sharply familiar. The pitch is the one used today.

Barnes's drawing is dated 1885, but there is a photograph of September 29 1881 which shows a different booth. Guy Higgins, a much more recent Punch & Judy man in Weymouth, commented on the frame's chequered cloth. He said that this meant the Punchman was an 'inland' performer who moved to the seaside to do the summer shows. The thick linen green-and-white cloths were used to cover hayricks in the fields. Such a cloth would make a sound cover for a booth.

There's even earlier evidence of a local Punch & Judy show to be found in the intriguing little pamphlet entitled *Sketches Written In, Round and About Weymouth*. Anonymous and undated, the booklet is believed to have been published in 1877. (Its author was a journalist on the *Southern Times* named Jarvis Harker.) Essay No III, 'Along the Esplanade', discusses some of the beach activities and concludes:

> I must now break off in the midst of a half-told story, leaving the policeman, the bathing-machine hack, the fortune-hunter, the itinerant discourser of discords, the Punch & Judy showman, the donkey-drivers, and a host of other personages and things undescribed.

57 First known photograph of a booth on the beach, 1881. The puppeteer is unknown.

Where had all these undescribed and disparate 'personages' appeared from? They – like their customers – had probably made the journey by rail. Railways were making accessible all manner of unlikely places, though they took their time with seaside Weymouth. Trains did not reach the town until 1857, ten years after they had arrived in Dorchester. Jeffery's *Illustrated Weymouth Guide* [1858] describes the much-delayed event with some gusto.

> Notwithstanding the various advantages, attractions and capabilities of Weymouth, it was not until Tuesday the 20th day of January, 1857, that this delightful and fashionable watering place possessed that indispensable requisite to the prosperity of a town, and the development of its resources – Railway communication.

Their arrival had taken so long that no one quite believed it when the Wilts, Somerset and Weymouth Railway announced the opening of the line. Not until a week later was the 'auspicious event' celebrated by the Mayor and Corporation, residents and visitors, accompanied by the band of the 15th regiment of Hussars. Banners 'flaunted gaily in the breeze' and a triumphal arch stretched from the Royal Terrace to the Esplanade. The railway terminus, designed by Brunel, was 320 feet long by 150 wide, and was made of wood, as was the detached Goods Shed, with a 'light elegant' roof, which was of glass. (What remained of this fine building was demolished – appropriately enough – in 1984.)

Before the arrival of the train, pioneering beach entertainers had encountered a fairly select audience. Around 1850 a London Punch & Judy man observed 'We generally goes into the country in the summer time for two or three months. Watering-places is werry good in July and August. Punch mostly goes down to the sea-side with the quality.'

The 'quality' had been joined by bank clerks and other white-collar workers who were beginning to enjoy an improvement both in wages and in their standards of living. Seaside holidays were widening their appeal, and the newcomers wanted to be entertained. The first of Weymouth's visitors had used the seaside as an extension of the inland spas, and expected similar attractions such as assembly rooms, circulating libraries, coffee houses and newspaper rooms, to which were added the further marine delights of promenades along the Esplanade, sea-bathing and the collecting of seaweeds and fossils. Now attention concentrated on the beach, as a playground for both adults and children, and new attractions were provided: some of them are still there today.

Excursion trains accelerated this change. They began to arrive in Weymouth shortly after the opening of the line. By April 1857, less than three months later, the *Dorset County Chronicle* was reporting on two excursion trains, one carrying around 200 people and the second, on a Monday, a 'monster' of eighteen carriages into which were packed a thousand trippers. Annual excursions soon became popular. The Great Western Railway company itself organised yearly trips from its centre at Swindon. By 1860 twenty trains a day were arriving and departing.

Then in 1871 the Bank Holiday Act became law, and many more people had the opportunity to visit the seaside. Excursion fares were lowered after 1873, with the result that in the season the town was crowded out with day trippers. If Weymouth had been closer to London (for years it remained the southern resort furthest from the capital) then there would have been even more visitors.

Excursion trains from 1880 were remembered by 'Octogenarian' writing in the *Dorset Daily Echo* in 1955. 'A great number of trains brought factory workers from the large towns for day trips. Some of them travelled all night, arriving about 8 o'clock, and they poured up through King-street to the sea front.' Stalls lined King Street, selling snacks and souvenirs, and impeding the access to the beach where the performers awaited them.

The majority of resorts had to cope with this problem as J.K.Walton has described: 'Between the station and their lodgings, or the sea, visitors almost everywhere had to run a gauntlet, contending with a motley crew of touts, hawkers, minstrels, bands, wandering showmen and stall holders. The more popular the resort, the greater the infestation…'

All manner of people tried their luck at the seaside. It was a free-for-all. In Miss Alice Hall's novel *Boys Together* [1888], Thurston Merriday, only child of a millionaire, takes an excursion train to Weymouth to seek his fortune, after being cut off by his father for refusing an arranged marriage. Incognito, Thurston joins the Wandering Minstrels as their piano player and lives as they do, from hand to mouth, performing on the beach in summer and in theatres and music halls in the winter. Well-heeled Merriday probably had no difficulty in finding himself a comfortable bed, but for other visitors accommodation became an urgent problem, as increasing numbers of people began to stay overnight.

This had happened before. When George III arrived in 1789, accommodation was so limited that some of the gentlemen in his entourage were forced to sleep in their carriages or stay in places as far away as Dorchester. The people of Weymouth were, as ever, quick to respond to this lack: by 1800 one in every seven dwellings was listed as a lodging house. The keepers were usually male, and likely to have other jobs as well. Later in the century, though, most of the keepers were women, in one of the few respectable occupations available to them.

The apartment system was commonly used. Visitors would rent a room or a suite, bringing their own food, while the landlady would do the cooking and cleaning. The Georgian houses along the Esplanade, formerly private dwellings, were slowly being developed into lodgings. According to John Meade Falkner, of all the terraces Belvidere was 'the last to fall'. Cheaper bed & breakfast accommodation could be found in the newly-built Park District and off Commercial Road.

All seaside resorts are afraid of being left behind in the rush to provide novelty and entertainment, and Weymouth has been no exception. Its infrastructure (or at least that of the Melcombe Regis side of town) was probably better than most, as the Corporation took overall charge of paving, lighting, sands and watchmen. Unusually, Weymouth Council owned the foreshore outright, which must have avoided a number of potential problems. Gas and water were privately provided.

What is surprising is that Weymouth has never had a serious pleasure pier, although the Stone Pier on the south side of the Harbour is one of the oldest in the country. The Harbour pier was built piece by piece as required and was known as the Pile Pier or Rubble Pier. It was rebuilt in 1840 and again in 1859, at a time when fanciful structures were advancing into the sea all round the coast, and was rented out to Weymouth & Portland Steam Packet Co., for local and Channel Island services. A Marine Walk along the pier was provided for visitors. A number of other proposals in the late nineteenth century, which involved a structure in the middle of the Bay, opposite the end of King Street, perhaps fortunately did not materialise. Belatedly, and with bizarre timing, the Pier Bandstand at the Brunswick Terrace end of the Esplanade was opened in 1939, and provided for a short-lived entertainment area. It proved something of a white elephant almost from the start. As with all piers, its upkeep was expensive, and the structure was demolished in 1986. The well-restored and rather elegant landside buildings are still in place.

Like Pierrot's, Punch's own journey took considerably longer than a short trip to the seaside. He has a rag-bag of origins, the principal one being – again like Pierrot's – the Commedia dell'Arte. He probably began there as a puppet, and has ended as one too. In Italy he was known as Pulcinella ('little chicken') because of his beaked nose and his clucking voice. His surname was Cetrulo (from *citrullo* – stupid). Predominantly a Neapolitan, he appeared in the plays as a *zanni* from the early seventeenth century onwards. His first known interpreter was Silvio Fiorillo, actor and dramatist, who also played Captain Matamoros, a rather similar character. Pulcinella already looked quite a lot like his descendant, with his huge beak and a harsh voice which anticipated the sound produced by the Punch & Judy man's mouth instrument, the swazzle. Pulcinella carried a cudgel, which he was not afraid to use; he was pot-bellied and sometimes hump-backed

58 *Pulcinella.*

– even doubly humped, which indicates his split personality and his ancient origins.

Like most of the characters of the Masks, Pulcinella's antecedents have been traced beyond the Commedia dell'Arte, to the Greek Dorian mime (from about 500BC) or Roman farce. The novelist George Sand (whose son Maurice became an authority on the Commedia) certainly thought that the latter was the source. She claimed that the character of Pulcinella derived from the Atellan Farce, performed in Italy from around the time of Christ's birth. The farces used a cast of stock characters, one of which was the bumpkin, Maccus, whom Sand claimed was a prototype of Punch.

Sand believed that a statue of Maccus in Rome, discovered in 1727, was proof of the connection. Maccus is seen 'equipped like his descendants with two enormous humps, a nose hooked like the beak of a bird of prey, and heavy shoes, tied about the ankle… The ancient type must have been somewhat baser and more hateful than the modern Pulcinella; provoking laughter chiefly by his deformities… I am confirmed in this opinion by the fact that in the Neapolitan farces two Pulcinellas are to be found: one is base and doltish, the veritable son of Maccus : the other is daring, thieving, quarrelsome, Bohemian and more of a modern creation.'

It's a neat and appealing theory, but not entirely convincing. Though there may be a connection, it is impossible to prove. Pulcinella is perhaps just a recurring human type, one which fits easily into many kinds of performance. He is an antagonist, a rebel, a figure who refuses to obey the rules. One of the strengths of folk art (frustrating though this might be for the historian) is that it can absorb influences from everywhere and anywhere. Further, it has been claimed by Punch expert George Speaight that in the Commedia Pulcinella was not hump-backed, or at least not consistently so. In 1618, he appears in a series of designs made from birds' feathers by Dionisio Minaggio (looking not unlike Pedrolino in his peasant garb). He does not have a hump in these portraits.

When the Commedia travelled to France, Pulcinella went with them, becoming a quick-witted French character, Polichinelle, who was hump-backed and ruffed. He grew plumper, more sophisticated and far more flamboyant in dress. He even went back to Italy in this garb (though he had remained his old self in Naples and Rome). In France, he became more famous as a marionette than as an actor, and more French than Italian in his behaviour. His squeaky voice was produced by the swazzle-like instrument known in France as the *sifflet-pratique* (usually shortened to *pratique*). When the Italian Players were expelled from France by Louis XIV, these puppets stayed behind. Small and insignificant, they could survive in a difficult world, out in the fairs, just as English puppets had survived during the Commonwealth when all other forms of theatre were rigidly banned. While other actors had been silenced, puppeteers were allowed to speak, though only through the *pratique*.

59 *Polichinelle.*

The greatest human Polichinelle was not to be seen until the nineteenth century. His name was Michel-Louis Vautrier (called Desiré) and he appeared, like the greatest of the Pierrots, on the stage of the Funambules in Paris.

When Punch first arrived in England it was in the shape of a puppet. There were three main types in use, and it's often impossible to tell which type was being employed in any given performance. There were the marionettes, the hand or glove puppets and the 'jigging' puppets, which were controlled horizontally by a central string. Puppets had thrived in Italy; the first known showman was a Sicilian. This is reflected in the extensive Italian vocabulary for puppetry. Generally, a marionette is a *fantoccio* and a glove puppet a *burattino* (from the Commedia Mask, *Buratino*). There is even a word – *fantocciata* – for a poor puppet show. In Italy the puppeteers used a *pivetta*, a tube of varying lengths inserted in the mouth to express the different voices of the *burattini*. (The word *pivetta* comes from *piva*, meaning 'bagpipe'.)

Puppets – or 'motions' as they were sometimes called – were of course nothing new to the England in which Punch appeared in the mid-seventeenth century (a libertine period which must have been much to his taste). Glove puppets had featured in Ben Jonson's play of 1614, *Bartholomew Fair*, set in London's Smithfield, where this most famous of English fairs was held. The puppets had probably been here since the Middle Ages. Between 1400 and 1550 they took part in the mystery plays, where they were used in the enactment of Bible stories. (Biblical themes continued to be used after the religious plays had fallen out of fashion. This led to some comic mixes of ancient and modern, as in the old routine where Punch pops his head up and casually addresses Noah, who is snug in his ark amidst the torrents, saying 'hazy weather, master Noah!')

Although they were old-established, puppets were still not necessarily welcomed everywhere they went. Puppeteers had fallen victim to the Elizabethan vagrancy acts and they continued to be suspected by the authorities. In 1630, for example, a band of puppeteers in Beaminster were denounced from the pulpit and then abruptly ordered to leave Dorset. They were regarded as an unwelcome distraction to everyday life:

> …the magistrates at Bridport observed a troupe of players who 'wander up and down the country with blasphemous shows and sights which they exercise by means of puppet-playing, not only by day but late in the night … so that the townsfolk cannot keep their children and servants in their houses'.

Conversely, the lowly puppets thrived during the Commonwealth period (1649–1660) when most other forms of theatre were banned. In 1660 Charles II returned from exile in France along with his assorted retinue and Punch's show may have come to England on the coat-tails of the restored King, in the form of the Italian marionettes which were more fashionable than the indigenous glove puppets. Better-documented is Samuel Pepys's first sight of Punch on May 9 1662 in the Piazza, Covent Garden – a day still commemorated by Punch & Judy puppeteers. Pepys mentioned the show in his diary and enjoyed it so much that he went on to see further performances. The puppeteer was an Italian known as 'Signor Bologna' (Pietro Gimonde) and his chief puppet was called Pollicinella. This would suggest that although the showman was Italian, the show itself had come from France. (There were so many variations on this puppet's name that it was no wonder that in England all the variants soon became shortened to Punch.)

Charles II gave his patronage to another Italian puppet player – probably a *fantoccini* man – who performed at Charing Cross or, more precisely at the top of Whitehall, where the statue of Charles I, hidden during the Civil War, now stands again. But the puppets' eminent respectability did not last for long. When James II was forced from his throne, the puppets went too. Punch and his kind had to retreat to the fairs and the village rounds. The writer Joseph Addison watched a puppet-theatre at such a fair and described it in bold, mock-heroic Latin couplets in a poem published in 1698. The Punch of the poem is massive and powerful. He dominates the action.

But there is one who lords it over all,
Whom we or Punch or Punchanello call,
A noisy wretch, like boatswains always hoarse,
In language scurrilous, in manners coarse;
Large is the buckle that his vest controls,
His mimic eye with living motion rolls,
His belly turgid of enormous size,
Behind his back a bulk of mountain lies.
His limbs a bulk and strength superior boast,
And uncontrolled he struts and rules the roost,
Chatters, and laughs immoderately loud,
And scolds and swaggers at the pygmy crowd.

Like Grimaldi the human clown, the Punch puppet combined elements of the Commedia with those of the English fool. A flexible character, he soon became full-bloodedly anglicised: a Punch instead of a Pulcinella. As Addison's lines show, by now Punch is growing larger than life, and becoming known as a character in his own right, one who appeared in the works of the leading writers of the day, and even had his name invoked in political controversies. He soon acquired an English wife (called Joan) and discarded his traditional white smock in favour of the English jester's red-and-gold motley. Punch's squeaker, too – his *pivetta* or *sifflet-pratique* – became known by its current name of 'swatchel' or 'swazzle'.

P.J.Stead summed up Punch's progress in the early eighteenth century.

> Punch made himself thoroughly at home in England. He has a wife, with whom he is destined to live unhappily ever after, and among the devils and jack-puddings of the fairs, he has found company which is extremely congenial. By his partici-pation in political controversy, he has anticipated the day when he will give his name to a national magazine. He has

also taken his place in our national artistic tradition. As a jovial and incorrigible evil-doer he has the voice of Pepys and Rochester, Addison, Steele, Swift and Gay, and of Hogarth and Henry Fielding.

Despite all this attention, Punch was still not yet the main character in all his shows. He was used as a clown who could step outside his role and comment on the action, just as another oversize figure, Shakespeare's Falstaff, could do. As a clown, he became (and continues to be) associated with puns, and he had already begun to take on the Devil. But at this point in his career he was not yet a violent character, neither beating his wife or bashing up bystanders. One of the reasons for this was practical. For a marionette, such actions were not technically possible: knock-about is a technique of glove-puppetry.

Punch began to take centre stage at the great Bartholomew Fair, held annually for three days at the end of August. He was announced by a fiddler, and was accompanied by one, too – or by a trumpet, or a drum. Peter Ackroyd has described how 'with his violence, his vulgarity and his sexual innuendo he was a recognisable urban character'. London had become his home. A glove puppet Punch is shown by Rowlandson (1785) beating the bare buttocks of his wife while George III and his Queen drive past on their way to Deptford. Punch also appeared at Southwark Fair, and is portrayed by Hogarth riding a stage horse which is busily picking a clown's pocket. Above is a poster advertising 'Punches Opera' and showing our hero 'wheeling his wife in a barrow towards the open mouth of a dragon'. He was also still appearing with his old Commedia companions. It was a rumbustuous age, and Punch was well-suited to it whether as human, glove-puppet or marionette.

The introduction to John Payne Collier's Punch & Judy script of 1828 includes a ballad which is said to date from the 1790s (although Collier probably wrote it himself). Its fourteen stanzas show what Punch had become, a figure who – apart from his lechery, displayed in a central section where he goes philandering in Italy and France, Germany and Spain – is familiar. He has a hump; he throws his child out of a window, tricks the hangman and defies the Devil.

PUNCH'S PRANKS

Oh! harken now to me awhile,
A story I will tell you
Of Mr. Punch, who was a vile
Deceitful murderous fellow:
Who had a wife, a child also, –
And both of matchless beauty;
The infant's name I do not know,
Its mother's name was Judy.
Right tol de rol lol, &tc.

But not so handsome Mr. Punch,
Who had a monstrous nose, Sir;
And on his back there grew a hunch.
That to his head arose, Sir;
But then, they say, that he could speak
As winning as a Mermaid,
And by his voice – a treble squeak, –
He Judy won, that fair maid.

But he was cruel as a Turk,
Like Turk, was discontented,
To have one wife – 'twas poorish work –
But still the law prevented
His having two, or twenty-two,
Tho' he for all was ready;
So what did he in that case do?
Oh! sad! – he kept a lady.

Now Mrs. Judy found it out,
And being very jealous,
She pull'd her husband by the snout,
His lady gay as well as.
Then Punch he in a passion flew,
And took it so in dudgeon,
He fairly split her head in two,
Oh! monster! – with a bludgeon.

And next he took his little heir,
Oh most unnat'ral father!
And flung it out of a two pair
Window; for he'd rather
Possess the lady of his love,
Than lady of the law, Sir,
And car'd not for his child above
A pinch of Maccabau, Sir.

His wife's relations came to town
To ask him of the cause, Sir;
He took his stick and knock'd 'em down,
And serv'd 'em the same sauce, Sir;
And said, the law was not his *law,*
He car'd not for a letter;
And if on him it laid its claw,
He'd teach it to know better.

[For the next four stanzas Punch proceeds on his amorous –
and murderous – travels.]

At last he back to England came,
A jolly rake and rover,
And pass'd him by another name,
An alias *when at Dover.*

But soon the police laid a scheme,
To clap him into prison:
They took him, when he least could dream
Of such a fate as his'n.

And now the day was drawing near,
The day of retribution;
The trial o'er, he felt but queer
At thought of execution.
But when the hangman, all so grim,
Declar'd that all was ready,
Punch only tipp'd the wink at him,
And ask'd after his lady.

Pretending he knew not the use
Of rope he saw from tree, Sir,
The hangman's head into the noose
He got, while he got free, Sir.
At last, the Devil came to claim
His own; but Punch what he meant
Demanded, and denied the same;
He knew no such agreement!

"You don't! (the Devil cried;) 'tis well,
I'll quickly let you know it;"
And so to furious work they fell,
As hard as they could go it.
The Devil with his pitch-fork fought,
While Punch had just a stick, Sir,
But kill'd the Devil, as he ought
Huzza! there's no Old Nick, Sir.
Right tol de rol lol, &tc.

As Punch's personality grew more defined, his position in society again began to slip, and it was from the fairs that the Punch & Judy show began to emerge – from among the dancing bears, slack-wire walkers, jugglers and other such creatures. The most famous puppet-master of the time was Flockton who was succeeded by Daniel Gyngell, a member of his company. Flockton's *fantoccini* included Punch, the Devil and a (live) Newfoundland dog. The Punch & Judy show evolved from the fairs into a form recognisable today during the years between 1760 and 1820 when the once-fashionable *fantoccini* had almost disappeared. Punch took to the streets as a lowly glove puppet – of necessity, as marionette shows were far less portable.

For cheapness' sake Punch puppeteers travelled alone, or with a companion bottler, one carrying the booth on his back and the other the box of puppets and a drum or trumpet to herald their performance. The show suited the streets, being fast-moving, quick-witted and dramatic, and the Punchman soon became a welcome and popular performer. His show, as George Speaight has pointed out, was a 'simple but fundamental reversal' of the previous marionette shows, in which Punch would pop up in scene after scene. As a glove puppet he remains on the stage, on the puppeteer's right hand, reacting to every event. The show was a straightforward procession of events to which Punch – by now having acquired a stick – responded with both wit and violence. There was a practical reason for the latter. For the showman, killing a character is the best way of ending one scene and going on to the next. This may sound crude, but holding the audience's attention while performing in a noisy street, full of movement, left no room for subtlety of interpretation. For ease of movement too, there were only four characters – Punch of course, with his wife, the Devil and a Doctor or Constable – the latter three representing matrimony, religion and the law – all of whom Punch succeeds in outwitting. George Speaight considered that:

Gradually upon this foundation a regular order of incidents grew up and new characters appeared; gradually an accepted 'drama' was adopted by all the showmen: a drama that has no author, for – as every puppeteer knows – the puppets have a way of imposing their actions and their own personalities upon the performance...a drama that is substantially still performed and still loved today.

The Punch & Judy show is, in fact, a last vestige of the Commedia dell'Arte in England, where the showman is free to improvise within an already determined structure.

Giovanni Piccini was the first Punch & Judy man about whom much is known. He was described in 1821 as 'a little thick-set man, with a red humorous-looking countenance. He had lost one eye, but

60 Sketch by Cruikshank of Piccini performing.

the other made up for the absence of its fellow by a shrewdness of expression sufficient for both. He always wore an oil-skin hat, and a rough great coat. At his back he carried a deal box, containing the *dramatis personae* of his little theatre; and in his hand, the trumpet...' Born in Italy, Piccini worked in London for many years and lived well on the proceeds, though he ended his days – drink his downfall – penniless and blind, in St. Giles Workhouse, Vinegar Yard. He died in 1835 and was buried in St. Pancras Churchyard.

After years of the oral tradition, Piccini's was the first performance to find its way into print, as *The Tragical Comedy, or Comical Tragedy of Punch and Judy.* John Payne Collier, a young, ambitious drama critic, transcribed the play in 1828 at the request of the publisher Septimus Prowett, while caricaturist George Cruikshank, who was later to illustrate some of the works of Charles Dickens, provided suitably grotesque impressions of the show. (Further and more charming illustrations of Piccini in action were published in a catalogue of Cruikshank's work which accompanied an exhibition of 1863.) Drawings and script have been a source of endless fascination. Piccini had originally performed in Italian until he acquired some grasp of English, when he adapted his play to suit an English audience. His broken English accent seems to speak through the pages:

> *Ladies and Gentlemen, pray how you do?*
> *If you all happy, me all happy too.*
> *Stop and hear my merry littel play;*
> *If me make you laugh, me need not make you pay.*

How much of the script is authentic, though, is impossible to say. Collier must have kept stopping Piccini's performance to make his notes, and he combined the collected text with a version he remembered from his childhood in Brighton. The text also has a curiously literary flavour, both in its language and in a number of its characters. Collier was a talented commentator who made some original contributions to English studies, but who is now remembered mainly as a fraud, particularly after his forgery of parts of a Second Folio of Shakespeare's plays. However, his reputation can mislead. The dream-like appearance of Nobody in Piccini's show might seem like one of Collier's inventions, but was actually part of the puppeteer's repertoire. Piccini, a great artiste, boasted of his skill in making the character remove his hat with one hand, a feat he claimed no other showman could perform.

Another unlikely character making a brief appearance is Pretty Polly, Punch's mistress. She has strayed from John Gay's immensely popular *Beggar's Opera*, which was a parody of the Italian opera fashionable at the time, and first performed in 1728. (A sequel of 1729 called – simply – *Polly*, was banned from the stage but became successful as a book.)

During the opera it's revealed that Polly Peachum has secretly married MacHeath, a highwayman who narrowly misses being hanged from 'the Triple Tree'. (The gallows earned this nickname because they were triangular in shape, with three supporting legs. Each of the three beams could hang eight people – enabling the simultaneous execution of twenty-four victims.) So entangled with women is MacHeath that he sees such a death as a merciful release and, like the rest of his gang of thieves, expects execution to be his ultimate and inevitable fate. He may have got away on this occasion, but in the end he will not escape.

That necessary agent, Jack Ketch the hangman, appears in both Collier's and Gay's plays, but this is only to be expected. Ketch,

61 Cover of The Beggar's Opera playscript.

62 Pretty Polly, with an admiring Punch, in a drawing by Cruikshank. The backcloth is an italianate garden.

born Richard Jaquet, had been a real and notorious executioner at Tyburn from the 1670s. It was he who beheaded the Duke of Monmouth after his failed rebellion. So feared was Ketch that his name became the generic term for a hangman through more than two centuries. When Punch is brought to execution for the murders he has committed, he feigns ignorance of the noose, asking the Hangman to show him what to do. This inevitably leads to the executioner being himself executed – by outwitting such a bogeyman Punch is a hero indeed. And to make the scene even more effective, the Hangman is given dangling legs like Punch's, enabling him to perform his grisly dance of death. (Executioners' ropes, incidentally, were made in Dorset, which gave rise to the expression 'being stabbed with a Bridport dagger'.)

The Tragical Comedy, or Comical Tragedy of Punch and Judy is an invaluable source which has been much reprinted. Collier certainly took the show seriously, providing learned footnotes about its origins. He was in fact the first person to point out the links between

63 *Jack Ketch carrying the gallows past a gaoled Punch, by Cruikshank.*

Punch & Judy and the Commedia dell'Arte in his introduction to the play, which regrettably is no longer included in modern editions of the text. There has been much debate as to how far Collier's script has influenced subsequent Punch & Judy performers. Since many Punchmen must have been illiterate, and often came from showmen families working within their own tradition, any influence must have been limited – especially since it's also said that Collier's script is impossible to perform.

More like a slice of performing life is the show which appears in the text of Henry Mayhew's *London Labour and the London Poor*, a series of interviews recorded around 1850, and published in 1856. Mayhew (1812–87) was a successful dramatist and prolific author who in 1841 was co-founder of *Punch, or the London Charivari*, a satirical magazine which in its early days was as subversive as the character after whom it had been named.

Remarkably, the showman Mayhew interviewed had bought both puppets and booth from the ailing Piccini (or 'Porsini' as he persistently called him). Piccini had brought them over from Italy, claiming that there was no one in England skilled enough to make such things. His characters were (in order of appearance) Punch – with a swivel eye, like his former master, Dog Toby, Scaramouch, Judy, Child, Pretty Polly, Nobody, Hector the Horse, Doctor, Servant, Blind Man, Constable, Officer, Jack Ketch and the Devil. Of these, Punch and Scaramouch came from the Commedia, while the Doctor may have derived from there or he might, like Hector the Horse, come from the English folk plays.

Although he'd acquired Piccini's puppets, Mayhew's showman didn't use all of them, and his show reflects his own character. He told Mayhew that Piccini was 'past performing when I bought my show of him, and werry poor'. Having never seen Piccini in action, he probably didn't know what to make of some of the puppets he'd acquired. In his version of the play, which he called *The Dominion of Fancy, or, Punch's Opera*, he had Punch, Judy, Baby, the Beadle, Merry Clown, Jim Crow, Ghost, Doctor, Jack Ketch ('or Mr. Graball'), Publican, Scaramouch and Satan. His clown outwits Punch with the help of a string of sausages, while a headless Scaramouch, in place of Nobody, does 'a comic dance, with his long neck shooting up and down'. Piccini's 'Servant in a foreign livery' becomes 'Jim Crow', from 'Jump, Jim Crow' which was the title of a song recently popularised by minstrel T.D.Rice. Rice's performance style was a gift to glove puppeteers because his song and dance routine 'relied largely on the upper part of his body'.

Mr. Punch christens a Magazine. The first cover of *Punch*, by A. S. Henning

64 Cover of the first issue of Punch magazine.

65 Mayhew's showman.

This was the third Punch & Judy show to appear in print, and was a different play from Piccini's. The second show to be published, in 1854, was called *The Wonderful Drama of Punch & Judy and their Little Dog Toby as performed to overflowing balconies at the corner of the street.* Illustrations were by 'The Owl' and the author is given as 'Papernose Woodensconce Esq.' (Journalist Robert Brough was both author and illustrator.) As might be guessed, this was intended for children, and is fast-moving and rather fantastically and self-consciously jokey, with characters who include a 'Gho-o-o-o-o-ost!' and a 'Horrid Dreadful Personage'. Punch historians are divided as to the value and authenticity of this show.

These three versions, produced within thirty years of one another, serve to illustrate how, within the framework of a series of confrontations with Punch, separate shows may emerge, depending on the showman and on his situation.

For some reason, Prince of Wales feathers had crested Piccini's booth and this tradition continued – in what became almost a parody of the Royal Patronage of Charles II. Mayhew's showman was dismissive of such a display. He remarked that 'Sometimes there's George and the Dragging, and the Rile Queen's Arms, (we can have them up if we like, cos we are sanctioned, and I've played afore rile princes). But anything for freshness. People's tired of looking at the Rile Arms, and wants something new to cause attraction, and so on.'

66 *Cover for the* Wonderful Drama of Punch & Judy, *1854.*

Inside Piccini's booth, the 'back scene', as depicted by Cruikshank, shows a gracious Italian garden with statues and topiary, which, as Mayhew's showman reported, is changed in the second part of the play. 'The back scene draws up, and shows the prison, with the winders all cut out, and the bars showing, the same as there is to a gaol…' This too is illustrated by Cruikshank. Later performers replaced the Italianate garden with a more English scene – just as pantomime settings became anglicised in Grimaldi's day. Weymouth Punch & Judy man Guy Higgins, for instance, often used a back scene of half-timbered houses for the introductory part of his show. He used a beach scene too, while performing on the sands. Frank Edmonds before him used a street scene from his native Chester.

67 Backcloth by Frank Edmonds.

Piccini's apprentice, who seems to have set up on his own before his impoverished master was forced to sell his puppets, was a man by the short, sharp name of Pike. He was an Englishman, like most of the Punch & Judy professors. (An honorary title, 'professor' – applied similarly in Italy – was first used in 1773. The puppeteer professes to perform to the best of his ability. Acrobats also use this title.) Pike is thought to be the first Punch showman in England to perform with a real dog. By 1817 the dog was called Toby, and there have been various suggestions for the name's origin. It may have been called after Tobias's dog in the book of his father Tobit in the Apocrypha; Toby was the English form of Tobias and the book was a favourite in the Middle Ages. It was also the slang word for a dog-handler, and this seems a more likely derivation. ('Toby' is not necessarily the dog's real name. He may have another one which is unknown to the audience, so that they cannot distract him during the show.) Mayhew's Punchman said that Pike's dog had been very enthusiastically received – 'a great hit it war'. So great was its success that some showmen had as many as three dogs performing. This could get a little out of hand!

Pike presumably worked his puppets in the same way as his master – by putting his first finger into the puppet's neck, with the second finger and thumb in the arms. This may sound obvious, but different methods were used in other countries. According to George Speaight, the Catalan system is 'three middle fingers in the shoulder-piece' and the French 'three outside fingers in the armpiece'. In an undated article, c.1900, on Guignol, the French equivalent of Punch & Judy, the puppets are described as having *'un mécanisme très simple: chacune d'elles cache sous ses vêtements une petite pince également en bois, aux deux branches de laquelle correspondent les bras: une légère pression sur la pince, et les bras se rapprochent'* – that is, the showman works the arms with a device like a pair of wooden scissors.

68 *Guignol in a Parisian park.*

A moment from Pike's show can be seen in an oil painting by Benjamin Robert Haydon called 'Punch or May Day' (1829) in the collection of Tate Britain in London. Here, the puppet booth is a corner of calm in a gusty, bustling scene with Marylebone Church in the background and a thoroughly pagan 'Jack-in-the-Green' well to the fore. Of the figures who pause to watch the performance, almost all are adults. Yet by the time of Robert Barnes's drawing of 1885, the majority of the watchers are children, as was increasingly the case. Like fairy tales, the Punch & Judy show has come to be regarded as a children's entertainment, a belief which has gradually imposed its own limitations on what is regarded by each generation as 'suitable' for a young audience. One of the reasons for the change was that in Victorian times, showmen were engaged by the middle classes to give performances in their houses, and often these engagements were for children's parties. Mayhew's showman remarked on the changes he was obliged to make to some of his performances.

> Some families where I performs will have it most sentimental
> – in the original style; them families is generally sentimental
> themselves. Others is all for the comic; and then I have to
> kick up all the games I can. To the sentimental folk I am
> obliged to perform werry steady and werry slow, and leave
> out all the comic words and business. They won't have no
> ghost, no coffin, and no devil; and that's what I call spiling
> the performance entirely. It's the march of hintellect wot's a
> doing all this…

Punch & Judy men say that, in the 1840s, Dickens invited a member of their fraternity to one of his soirées. The Punchman was paid a fee for his performance – the first fee ever to be paid for such a show, which generally depended on a bottler to extract money from the crowd. The shows became a fashionable fixture in London society.

Dickens loved the grotesqueries of Punch & Judy, and they make their first fictional appearance in his novel *The Old Curiosity Shop* amongst the giants, dwarfs, stilt-walkers and waxworks. Little Nell and her grandfather encounter the 'exhibitors of the freaks of Punch', Codlin & Short, in a graveyard, repairing the puppets which lie scattered on the grass. This is a most appropriate spot, as showmen believe they have the right to perform in any churchyard – and traditionally, the Punch & Judy man is buried with his puppets. Codlin & Short's Punch, meanwhile, remains 'perched cross-legged up on a tombstone behind them … his nose and chin as hooked and his face as beaming as usual'. Punch, frighteningly, never rests.

Indoor bookings were welcomed by the showmen, as street performances were hard work and often unlucrative, and they must have been willing to adapt their performances for this different audience. They had left the fairground behind them – Pike was

69 Punch in the churchyard. Illustration by Cruikshank for The Old Curiosity Shop *by Charles Dickens.*

perhaps one of the last Punch & Judy men to exhibit at fairs – and they may have wished to leave the streets behind them too.

Although they did not entirely disappear, at least not from London. In their massive enterprise, *London, a Pilgrimage* (1872), Gustav Doré and Blanchard Jerrold describe a performance of the street-folk's 'national comedy theatre'. The audience are drawn as they were to Piccini and Pike by the music of the *pipares* or pan pipes: sounds produced by blowing across the top of a series of graduated reeds. (These were usually accompanied by a drum.) The performance is well received, but there is an elegiac note to the description of it. Photographs show that street performances survived in London well into the twentieth century, but by the end of the Second World War they were becoming something of a rarity. Punch had moved away, he had gone to the coast to taste the sea air.

The Punch & Judy Show

I never get bored ... the only man that got bored was Mr. Punch. Many a time he's been very bored with me, he's looked down on me and said, 'You're a silly old sod, you are, you know.'

Frank Edmonds in conversation with Robert Leach, 1978

70 *Bathing machines, in a photograph by Edwin Seward.*

FRANK EDMONDS WAS Weymouth's Punch & Judy man for fifty years and Dawn Gould still remembers him vividly. Her mother ran the bathing machines and taught swimming, so Dawn was brought up on the beach every summer from 1927 to 1939. 'We were on the sands from 6.30 each day and were part of a closely knit working community,' she remembered. The bathing machines consisted of two large huts, one for men and one for women, and a row of striped singles. By the 1920s mixed bathing had been allowed, but swimmers still had to change under cover and there was a strict dress code. Men had to wear one-piece bathing suits, with a skirt across the front to protect their modesty.

A few years before the rules had been much stricter. In *The Dorset Coastline* Llewellyn Pridham describes being taken for a 'dip' by his maiden aunt 'during the post-victorian period'. A numbered ticket was bought from a kiosk 'surrounded by blowing clothes-lines, supporting the towels and costumes of the more careless folk who had not brought their own'. The machines were lined up on the sands and hauled by a carthorse out into deep water. For bathing, his aunt wore a costume of thick serge, combining 'both bloomers and knee-length skirt', the whole being kept in place by elastic at wrist and ankle. 'In addition, to lend it elegance, it was trimmed with red and white tape and sported a deep sailor collar.' Such precautions seem rather excessive, given that mixed bathing was not yet allowed and 'a clear fifty yards' separated male and female bathers.

Even in those days, the tram lines which led from the two great saloons down to the sea were warped and rusted by salt water. 'It must have been quite a spectacle to see these monstrosities moving majestically towards the ocean; gaily painted, decked with bunting, thronged with the prospective bathers', Pridham imagined.

Renting out the machines was still a good way to earn money in the 1920s. Dawn Gould's mother had an 'office' in a spare bathing machine which was close to Frank Edmonds' pitch, so the little girl had every opportunity to watch the puppet show.

> My very best friend was Dog Toby, and he and I were together all day. He was a small long-haired black & white terrier, who looked like a miniature collie. He was bathed every day and had a clean red/white/blue frilly collar each day. His fur was like silk. He would sit proudly on the left hand side of the 'set' and never move a muscle. He was <u>always</u> called Dog Toby and <u>never</u> just Toby. Frank would do some marvellous scenes, some of which I have <u>never</u> seen elsewhere. There was a

boxing ring, with a black and a white boxer, and as they got 'tired' they would do a most fantastic slow-motion fight, which was wonderful to see. Frank also had a 'troupe' of Chinese plate-spinners. The plates would spin for ages and would be thrown from one performer to another, and I never saw one drop, ever. The Beadle, in a wonderful gold-braid uniform, would have a deep sonorous voice and was awfully scary. He made several threats 'off-stage' before he finally popped up, and we kids <u>hated</u> him. Joey the Clown was very much on stage and poor Baby Punch was put through torture! We all put a penny in the bag when the 'bottler' came round.

Piccini's pupil Pike was thought to be the first showman in England to use a live dog in a Punch & Judy show. Previously, stuffed dogs had been used. Live dogs were very popular with the crowds, but could be unreliable. Frank Edmonds' Dog Toby was well-behaved and kept in a condition worthy of a Cruft's canine; his master evidently had

71 Some of Frank Edmonds' puppets.

high standards in all aspects of his craft. Silvia Noakes, born in Weymouth in 1932, remembers that Frank stored his booth in the garage of the New Cooper's Arms in Maiden Street, where her grandfather was landlord.

> In the spring Mr. E. would check over the puppets and paint and repair them as required. I would sit on his knee, and he would practise his various voices. The work would take him several weeks. He did everything himself including sewing repairs. I remember even then feeling lucky in having a Punch and Judy show all to myself.

Minor repairs were done weekly. In the 1970s Edmonds told an *Echo* reporter 'Every Sunday morning I repair them, put new braid on the dresses and paint them, fresh for the next week.' Traditionally, the showmen make all their own puppets and Frank, like his father and grandfather before him, was no exception. True Punchman that he was, Frank made everything himself.

Despite being made of tough materials like oak and leather (Mr. Punch weighed seven and a half pounds), the puppets, seventeen of them, took 'quite a hammering'. Leather was used for cheeks, eyebrows and lips, which were then painted over. (Frank's colours could be garish, even by the exuberant standards of the genre.) The noses of the more feisty characters were made from a separate piece of wood, inserted into the face and held by a nail, so that they could be replaced when necessary.

Like his puppets, Edmonds' booth was heavy, and must have been hard work to shift about. Punch & Judy man Martin Bridle (Professor Allsorts) who was brought up in Weymouth and as a child watched Edmonds perform, described a special feature of the frame.

> One of the things about Frank Edmonds' booth was that down the sides of the proscenium facing into the acting

area he had what were essentially two very long slapsticks [a flexible pair of paddles]. They were loose, held just at the top by a pin so when a head hit the side you got a resounding crack. He used this to great effect with the boxing match and also during the Punch & Judy fight.

Frank's father, Harry, had also been a travelling Punch & Judy man, performing at the seaside in the summer and on the road in the winter. Seaside pitches could be lucrative, and this sometimes led to bitter competition for space. Once, Harry's show on the Isle of Man was burnt down by angry pierrots, jealous of his popularity. Harry at some point in his life went to sea as a cook, and spent his spare time on board carving wooden figures: he never really stopped being a puppeteer. He provided twelve Punch & Judy shows for the Coronation route in 1902, and performed in Australia and New Zealand.

Frank began working with Harry when he was ten years old (and therefore under age). He remembered his father as a 'very, very good showman, one of the best'. He told Robert Leach that he could watch his father's show 'and laugh and laugh and laugh'. In the off-season, the show would be installed in an upstairs room of the family's furniture shop in Chester, and Frank used to do his own performances there. His first solo public performance occurred when Harry was suddenly taken ill before an important engagement.

Frank left school at the age of thirteen, and a few days later was on the road. He kept one of his grandfather's puppets and used his father's 'script' (which he would have learnt by ear). In 1959 he said that he was still using his father's sixty-year-old version of the show.

His brother Claude, too, followed in the family tradition, inheriting his father's puppets and performing in Whitby for more than twenty years. Latterly, he bottled for his brother in Weymouth, and conducted sing-alongs with the children in the audience, including numbers such as 'Puppet on a String' and 'Grandad' (as Pam Brady in the nearest beach stall still recalls). He is thought to have performed with his brother too – this was possible, as the booth was a large one.

Frank Edmonds was probably one of the last Punch & Judy men to travel the country, which he did for many a long year. He walked up to twenty miles a day, accompanied by his bottler and sometimes Dog Toby as well, pushing his booth on a handcart and sleeping under it with a couple of blankets, or else in a haystack. Of these days he remarked to Robert Leach, 'A rolling stone gathers no moss – as you earn a couple of bob, you go and spend it in a pub.'

Edmonds was on the road from February to May, and then at the seaside until September when he returned to the road. In December he went home, to perform at the Christmas parties. After the First World War, he bought a five-seater Ford car and adapted the back so that he could sleep in it. Edmonds became Weymouth's Punch & Judy man in 1926, performing up to seven shows a day – and often double that number on Bank Holidays. He found the job almost by chance, as Guy Higgins recounted to the *Dorset Echo* in 2004.

> Frank Edmonds told me that before the Second World War there were changing tents lining the bottom of the sea wall – at that time the sand had not been bulldozed to the present level. He originally came to Weymouth to travel on the ferry and discovered that the Punch & Judy man at the time was notoriously unreliable, largely due to the desire for thoracic lubrication – he liked a drink.
>
> This man could usually be found in one of two places, the Gloucester Arms or one of the vacant changing rooms. His booth consisted of four bamboo poles, some canvas to go around them, and his puppets.
>
> When a family wanted a show, they would have to ask the beach superintendent to find the Punch & Judy man and he would come to them, set up his booth and do the show. Once paid, he would leave everything where it was, go to the Gloucester and get drunk.

At lunchtime closing the now legless performer would be carried on to the sands and dumped in a vacant changing tent, then when another show was required someone found him, retrieved his props from where he had left them and sobered him up.

A performer with less of a desire for thoracic lubrication than his predecessor would obviously have been warmly welcomed – and Frank Edmonds was much more than that. Martin Bridle said it was only later he realised just how good and how funny Frank was. He often drew huge crowds, to whom he made little concession, beyond adding either the plate-spinners or boxers to the performance.

Robert Leach recorded some of Frank's show which opened, traditionally, with Punch and his obliging Dog Toby.

> *Toby sits on the playboard as the show starts. Punch comes up, dances round singing, and bumps into him.*
>
> **Punch** Oo, oo, my long lost dog Toby, hello, Toby, shake hands, shake hands.
>
> *Toby does so, first with one paw, then with the other. Punch then gets Toby to sit up and, using the slapstick, Toby 'shoulders arms'. Punch dances round again, when up comes 'Toby's Man', who also bumps into Toby.*
>
> **Toby's man** Oo, my long lost Toby, how long have I lost you?
>
> **Punch** Your Toby? He's my Toby.
>
> *He hits Toby's man with a stick so that he falls flat on the stage. Toby puts his paw out and lifts him up.*

After further argument, Punch appeals to the audience, who always say that the dog is Punch's ('Course they do,' said Frank). There follows a contest of skill, during which the dog always obeys Toby's man and never Mr. Punch. Then Toby's man appeals to the audience who now admit that it's 'Yours!'

Punch then offers to fight for it. Of course, Toby joins in the fight, which ends with him getting Punch's nose between his teeth and carrying him off.

As well as Dog Toby, Punch, Judy and Baby, Frank's characters included the Beadle (a Dickensian figure preferred by him to the Policeman), Joey the Clown, who like Grimaldi, does business with a string of sausages, the Ghost and Jim Crow. Jim introduced himself with the words 'Hello boys and girls, I'm Jim Crow, C.R.O.W. – Crow'. A likeable and amusing chap, he would sing 'Polly Wolly Doodle' and 'I Come From Mississippi'. As the surviving Jim Crow puppet has feet, it seems probable that he danced as well. While he sang, the Crocodile would sidle up to sit beside him, watching the singer's waving hands with a beady eye, until the moment when he could pull one of them into his open jaws. There was also a Doctor, who had been called Dr. Jollop by Harry Edmonds – 'jalop' being the Victorian word for a laxative. Frank dropped this joke, as being unsuitable for his pre-dominantly child audience. This puppet became Dr. Jeremy Catchem.

Frank still had a Hangman, though not a Devil. Instead he had a Bogeyman, because he had been told that 'you shouldn't call the Devil'. The Bogeyman ended Frank's show. Defeated by Punch, he rolls along the playboard, 'roly-poly, roly-poly' until Punch whirls him away with his stick.

> Now, ladies and gentlemen, that's the end of the performance, thanking you one and all, how do you do, how do you do, and how do you do.

Frank also had set pieces within the show, which were both an extra treat for his audience and an attraction to casual passers-by. These were the black and white boxers and the Chinese jugglers, demonstrations of his manual dexterity. (He had, too, a more unusual character called Knockabout, with a red nose and a tartan jacket, who was probably a drunk.)

72 Punch twirling the Devil, by Cruikshank.

Above all, of course, he had Mr. Punch, with whom he had a strong relationship. Punch, he said, seemed alive to him. 'Some days he'd be just like me with a bad head. "What's the matter with you today, Mr. Punch? Was you on the beer last night?" "No, I wasn't on the beer last night." We used to play hell with each other.' Edmonds enjoyed such bickering. 'Of course, it was me all the time,' he said, 'but still, I never used to think that.'

In the 1930s Frank was still on the road in the off-season. The modern fairs with their hurdy-gurdies and grinding machinery were too noisy, but race meetings could be profitable:

> on one rainy day in Cattistock [a hunt village about sixteen miles north of Weymouth] ... he set up the booth, put Toby in front of it and collected £5-17s without unpacking a puppet. The racegoers saw the wet dog and – '"Oh, what a beautiful dog, buy him a bone" – pound note; "What a lovely little dog" – handful of silver,' and so on.

When interviewed in 1959 he said that he could no longer afford to stay in Weymouth all winter, and so he returned home to Chester where he owned a hardware shop. He lived in a caravan at Wyke Regis from Whitsun to the end of September, which he shared with his bottler, barker and nephew, Sidney Edmonds. At some point too he had an antique shop in Weymouth – he was certainly not a showman for the money. A Punch & Judy man's income is erratic and unpredictable.

Like many a trade, Punch & Judy has its secrets. Edmonds told Robert Leach something of the showman's cant, or 'parlary' which they spoke among themselves. This derives from a mixture of Italian and costermongers' slang, dating back to the eighteenth century, when it was used by actors in the fairgrounds. Frank said that he had 'picked it up here and there... When you're on the road, you meet up with different people, you go into a pub, start talking... "How was the collection?" They'd turn around to you, "Oh, nanti medzies", meaning, literally, no money. Silver they call "snow", a "bionc'" or a "deaner" is a shilling, a "clod" a penny. An "omi" is a man, and his wife is a "mozzy". The cant is dying out now, though it has survived to some extent among the gay community – notably in the 1960s in the radio show 'Round the Horne'.

This arcane language hadn't changed much in a hundred or so years. In *London Labour and the London Poor* (1856) the Punch & Judy man told Henry Mayhew '"Co. and Co." is our term for partner, or "questa, questa", as well. "Ultray cativa", – no bona [good]. "Slumareys" – figures, frame, scenes, properties. "Slum" – call, or unknown tongue. "Ultray cativa slum" – not a good call. "Tamboro" – drum; that's Italian. "Pipares" – pipes. "Questra homa a vadring the slum, scarper it, Orderly." – there's someone a looking at the slum. Be off quickly. "Fielia" is a child; "Homa" is a man; "Dona" a female; "Charfering-homa" – talking-man, policeman. Policeman can't interfere with us, we're sanctioned.'

At the centre of the mystery is the 'swatchel' or 'swazzle'. This mouth instrument, used to make Punch's voice, was known to Edmonds as 'the call'. Dawn Gould remembers how before he started his act, Frank would sing gently to himself, 'I'm Forever Blowing Bubbles' or 'Just a Song at Twilight' with his swazzle in his mouth. Every now and again he would ask, 'Are you ready, Mr. Punch?' and Punch, shilly-shallying, would reply, 'I'm putting on my trousers' or 'I'm buttoning my jacket.' Then all at once he would pop up in his red and gold glory, and the show would begin. (This repartee with Mr. Punch before the show was an old tradition. Frank may have been one of the last Punch & Judy men to use it.)

Punch & Judy men are still reluctant to go into any details about the swazzle. Mayhew's showman was careful to give only a partial explanation of it. He produced 'a small flat instrument, made of two curved pieces of metal about the size of a knee-buckle, bound together with black thread'. He wouldn't reveal the metal's composition, saying only that it was not zinc or tin, as both of these were poisonous. Learning to use the call had taken him six months; he had been taught by Piccini how to work it from the soft palette because his own master had refused to teach him. Learning the technique had been hard, but now, he said, he was as proficient as anyone. The instrument is used for Mr. Punch's voice, so in showman cant he is called the 'swatchel', while the Punch & Judy man is the 'swatchel omi'. Attempts to discuss the swazzle are generally discouraged. Professor John Styles told a story about a journalist who unsuccessfully tried one out. Nervously, he asked the Punchman what would happen if he swallowed it. 'Eat plenty of plum pudding and it'll come out the other end,' replied the showman. 'Have you ever swallowed one?' asked the journalist. 'Yes,' replied the Punchman, 'the one you've just tried.'

Many showman will not allow their shows to be transcribed or videoed, though Frank Edmonds seemed unconcerned by the implications of this kind of seaside piracy. Once when asked by a Punchman if he could record the show, Edmonds replied 'I don't mind, you please yourself. I lead, follow who can!'

Secretive, itinerant, the Punch & Judy men kept themselves to themselves. Although they were charged for their pitches they, like the donkeys, were disregarded by the powers-that-be, who did not seem to

73 Donkey-riding by Edwin Seward.

realise just how valuable their contribution to beach life was. Neither puppets nor donkeys (nor goats) were considered worthy of mention in Weymouth's annual publicity brochure (first published in 1901) until after the Second World War. Yet both Punch and the donkeys are still there on the beach, long after most other entertainers have vanished. Both are mentioned in the *Sketches* of 1877, and by Llewelyn Powys in his recollections of the beach in 1888 – the latter year being incidentally the date when it's noted in the official records that John Downton, Eli Roper and John Spencer Bleathman had applied for permission from the Corporation 'to place donkeys on the sands'.

John Downton's son Jack was on the beach at the age of ten, and Jack's son Len followed his father and grandfather in the business. When he was interviewed by the *Echo* in 1965, Len Downton had eighteen donkeys on Weymouth sands, many of them imported from Ireland, where their lives had most likely been harder. Donkeys are suited to beach work; the sand acts as an abrasive and is good for their hooves. In 1945, at least, they had a statutory lunch-hour. 'Donkeys stop work 1–2pm' the *Echo* reported. The donkeys usually wintered together on a farm, kicking their heels in the green fields, where Len reckoned they could 'look after themselves with reason'. Glimpses of brushes with officialdom can sometimes be found too. In 1923 it was proposed to move them to 'the North side of the Bond Street site'. Regarding this proposal, one Weymouth councillor remarked that as 'they had been going in one direction for 400 years it would need the whole strength of the Council with a bunch of carrots to induce them to go the other way'. For some years they were so popular an attraction that there were three donkey stands. The Downton donkeys finally retired in 2000, but since 2005 others have been working on the beach.

The last heyday of both donkeys and puppets – two perennially popular entertainments – was the 1950s, when tourists were still choosing to take their holidays at the English seaside rather than abroad, just before the age of package tours and cheap flights to warmer shores. This was the time of what is now regarded as the

74 Frank Edmonds performing in 1957, by Revd Tanner. The Marilyn Monroe figure (probably by Fred Darrington, most famous of Weymouth's sand sculptors) comes as a surprise in an age when bikinis were still banned from the beach.

traditional seaside holiday, a time of kiss-me-quick and candy-floss, fish-and-chips and Punch & Judy.

Many Dorset people can recall the Punch & Judy show in the 1950s. Bonny Sartin of The Yetties folk group remembers trips down the line from Thornford: 'we had three village outings, the Sunday School, the Bell Ringers and the Cricket Team, so we must have seen the show three times a year.' For him, 'a summer beach without Punch, Judy, the Policeman and the Crocodile doesn't seem right'. (A song in The Yetties' repertoire, 'The Punch & Judy Man' is actually about Cleethorpes and not Weymouth.)

Punchman John Styles remembered that Frank's show could run for three quarters of an hour and contained 'lots of business' including Punch and Toby 'practising on a big punchball on elastic which was hilarious'. Toby would duck, and the ball would, of course, hit Punch on his prominent nose. He remembered a Doctor, too, 'bald headed and minuscule beside the others. When Punch hit it, its hands would come up either side of its head and it would vibrate like a bell.'

John Stockley's father Len ran the height and weight machine on the beach and so, like Dawn Gould, young John spent most of his summers by the sea. As a boy in the 1950s, he watched many of Frank's performances. A rather unapproachable man, Frank would dissociate himself from his show. It was nothing to do with him: the puppets were responsible for what happened.

He was however friendly with Len Stockley. Frank had a dry sense of humour (and, incidentally, a beautiful speaking voice). Some of his more subtle jokes went over the heads of his audience. John remembers the pair commiserating with each other on the tight-pursed nature of the 'blue rinse brigade' who visited the resort in September, after the children had gone back to school. Not a lot of profit could be made out of them: they were 'all pound notes and knickers, and they don't change either of them'.

John Stockley also recalled that Frank used the same puppets over and over again, relying on his repairing skills to keep them going. His Judy in particular was 'well-battered'. Like many people, John Stockley

75 Frank Edmonds and his bottler Sid Baldwins.

remembers Frank Edmonds with great affection. For years after Frank retired, visitors would ask Professor Guy Higgins for news of him.

By the end of the 1960s, English seaside towns had begun to slide slowly into a decline – from which some resorts have never recovered. For Frank Edmonds, who by 1959 was having to make changes in order to survive financially, there were also some more private disasters. In June 1964, Frank's nephew and assistant, Sidney Edmonds, died in Weymouth Hospital. (He was replaced as bottler by Sid Baldwins.) Then in August 1966 his daughter Sylvia and son-in-law Michael Krol were killed in a car crash, and so Frank and his wife decided to move into the couple's Chester home in order to look after their two young grandchildren, orphaned by the crash.

In 1969, he sold his booth and puppets to a Weymouth antique dealer, and appeared to have given up performing. However, the next year he was back, with a new booth and a fresh set of puppets. Frank Edmonds did not finally retire until 1976, after fifty years as Weymouth's Punch & Judy man. He was almost seventy-three years old and the show had been his life. As he said, 'I never begrudged a second of it, I was always glad to have been a Punch & Judy man.'

Tracing Frank Edmonds' predecessors on the beach is a decidedly more difficult matter. Professor Murray was Weymouth's first known Punch & Judy man, who was there from the 1880s to 1912.

76 Painting: Horse Racing on Lodmoor, by an unknown artist. One Punch & Judy booth is being carried across the foreground, while a second is to the left.

A photograph of 1881 shows a plainish frame with a check cloth, which may be what Murray used when he first arrived in Weymouth, or which may have belonged to a different performer. There were, of course, other Punch & Judy men around – and had been for some time. A painting in Weymouth Museum, entitled 'Horse Racing and Fair at Lodmoor' is dated c.1870 (though the costumes look slightly earlier). A man with a booth, a boy carrying a box of puppets and a woman can all be seen making their way together across the painting's centre, while to their right another Punch & Judy show is in progress.

In 1887, when all sorts of celebrations were being held for Queen Victoria's Jubilee, there was a Punch & Judy show in the park at Winterborne Herringston, just south of Dorchester. Two carefully-composed photographs remain as souvenirs of the show (one plain, one coloured). The booth, decorated partly with stencilled designs, is not as carefully crafted as Professor Murray's, who apparently made a new booth for that year, and is probably the work of an itinerant showman, making the most of a golden season.

Such lowly persons were disregarded by guidebooks and newspapers, and the main sources of information for the early history of Punch in Weymouth are the Borough Records, and in particular the minutes of the Amusement Committee (a body which intermittently changed its name and grouping, and which became the Entertainments Committee). The minutes confirm that in 1904 permission was granted 'to James Murray to perform with Punch & Judy on the sands free of charge'. As seen in an Edwardian postcard, his frame was an elaborate one. 'Murrays Pulchinello' it declares and underneath the dates '1906 … 1887'. Then 'Garden Parties Attended'. Harlequin and Pierrot, a dashing pair, lounge at each side of the frame, and below them Punch is teaching the alphabet to a monkey. There seems to be a live animal on the playboard: another monkey or perhaps a muzzled dog (in compliance with the anti-rabies regulations). These features sound promising, and the show seems to have been a good one, since by 1907 (when beach sites were becoming increasingly lucrative) Murray was tendering £1 for his pitch, as he still was in 1912.

77 *Punch & Judy in Winterborne Herringston park, 1887, by William Miles Barnes. The Punchman is not known.*

In 1989 the elderly Punchman Fred Tickner recalled seeing Murray's show on Weymouth beach in 1910. He said it was a very good show, 'colourful and everything'. He may be the only person who has left any record, however scanty, of Murray's performances in Weymouth.

Records show that a J. Murray performed in Paignton in 1913 (where he paid only a shilling a week for his pitch) and this was most probably the same man. Certainly, in 1914 the Weymouth Amusement Committee approved the resolution 'Mr. Maggs to have the Punch and Judy Show on the Sands as in previous years' which might suggest this was not his first season. Six generations of Maggs have been Punch & Judy men; this family member was Joseph. He had begun performing at the age of ten, and appeared in Sanger's Circus. He came up from Cornwall in 1910 to become Bournemouth's Punch & Judy man but, according to Hazel Maggs, he left that pitch around 1914 when the charges looked like becoming too expensive, and went to Weymouth instead. Joseph was also a travelling showman, and was described as such on his son Philip's birth certificate. This was a heavy task, as he did not use a cart, carrying the booth on his shoulders – until the day

78 *Professor Murray's booth, c.1906.*

he bought a donkey for the cost of a drink and half a crown. When Joseph died in 1934, his wife wanted the figures burnt. Instead, they were stored in the attic and used by their son Bill, the first of their five sons to take up the show.

Robert Leach has described in some detail the Maggs' show, which goes back at least as far as the first half of the nineteenth century:

> In this, Punch is a 'terrible old man' who kills his wife and child. When the beadle arrives to apprehend him, he beats him about the head and runs away to join a travelling circus. It is here that the clown, Jim Crow, the crocodile, the plate-spinners, boxers and other entertainers are found. Their interludes are interspersed with a scene when the ghost of Judy haunts Punch, and another when Punch makes a pact with the devil, selling his soul to buy more time. In the end the law catches up with him and though there is some possibility that the original Maggs' show saw Punch hanged, within memory he has always hanged the Hangman. This story has strong affinities with that of Faust, which featured in eighteenth century puppet shows and pantomimes, though it appears to have died out around 1800.

In Weymouth, 1914 was a 'disastrous season' in a disastrous year for the world. Whether Maggs stayed on any longer is not recorded, but 1915 sounds to have been even worse, according to the Borough records. The Concert Platform performances were terminated before the end of the season; there were lighting restrictions – and very few visitors. The Amusement Committee were forced to turn their attention landwards to such practicalities as allotments during this very short season.

Records are scanty for the rest of the war and its aftermath. In 1920 B.J.Staddon, member of another Punch & Judy dynasty, was asked to submit a tender, and in 1921 the minutes state that a beach site was let for Punch & Judy at a rate of ten shillings per week. Though mainly

79 Bert Staddon's booth, 1922. Master-copy for a new postcard.

connected with Weston-super-Mare, the family also performed at Bournemouth and Boscombe. In 1922 a new postcard was produced of the Staddon booth on the beach and the records state that an unspecified Punch & Judy man was renting the pitch.

In 1923, 'Mr. C.North' was offered the pitch at a rate of £1 per week. This was presumably Claude North, Clacton's showman, who was still touring the country in the 1930s on his ingenious machine – 'a motorized tricycle with his show built on to the back'. Professor North refused the pitch at that price, and Bert Staddon took it on at his old rate.

As a child, Punchman John Alexander saw Claude North perform in Clacton. In 1993 he described the show as 'splendid' and 'old fashioned with all the bits'. There was 'a lot of byplay with the Clown, very reminiscent of the Harlequinade'. North's bottler, probably his brother, was 'very active', pursuing any passing trade up the nearby cliff paths.

The story goes that one day he got right to the top of the cliff and there were two men standing there talking with their backs to the sea. He rattled the bag and asked for a contribution. They said, 'Well, we're not looking mate,' to which he replied, 'Well, the dog is!' There was the dog, sitting behind them watching. They coughed up apparently.

Bert Staddon did not stay much longer in Weymouth. In September 1924, Council members agreed that 'Mr. Beavis be granted a Beach site for "Punch & Judy" show on the following terms – June 10s per week, July 15s, August £1, September (3 weeks) £1'. In 1926, he was charged a flat rate of £15 and in 1929 he was again charged £15 and given a three-year lease. Then in March 1930 a letter was read to the Committee from a Mr. P.Carcass 'asking for permission to perform "Punch and Judy" on the Sands during the 1930 Season, together with particulars and terms.'

As Mr. Beavis had written stating it was not his intention to perform at Weymouth this season, the Committee decided that subject to satisfactory references and terms, to grant a permit to Mr. Carcass.

This would have been Philip Carcass (also known as P.H.Coleman) another showman from a family of puppeteers, which dated back many years. It's said that their origins were Neapolitan. In a survey of 1881, Walter and Mary Carcass, aged twenty-three and eighteen respectively, are listed as Punch & Judy showmen living in Horsham. Though H.A.Carcass introduced the show to South Africa in 1911, the family had become Sussex-based and a glimpse of their local show is provided in an article in the *Brighton Gazette* in 1936:

On the beach the Punch and Judy show was run by a Professor Carcass – I notice the same name on the present one so perhaps it is a family concern. I can well remember the old professor and his wife, a clean homely body in a red shawl and rigid-fronted bonnet.

There was an orchestra too in those days, supported by a man who banged a drum and played the panpipes fixed round his neck-cloth; at intervals carrying on a dialogue with Mr. Punch in which the latter usually scored.

According to an account by Walter Wilkinson in *Puppets through Lancashire*, in 1936 the performer would have been Carcass's seventy-four-year-old grandfather. In that year, Wilkinson watched Philip Carcass perform on Blackpool beach at one of the three Punch & Judy pitches on the sands.

He handles his puppets with assurance, and his Toby is a deft assistant. His Punch is a joyous fellow who chuckles continually, and in all his slap-stick Mr. Carcass contrives a spirited rhythm. It was interesting to see one of the figures lift a hand and remove its hat, a trick which I have never seen before, but which is mentioned in that Covent Garden show, which Cruikshank portrayed, as being the trick which had lifted this particular showman above his rivals.

The letter stating Professor Carcass's intentions is unfortunately no longer in existence, and it's unclear whether he did appear in Weymouth or not. More importantly, it is unclear when Frank Edmonds began to perform on the beach. His name first appears in the minutes of October 1932 with a tender of £45 p.a., which was accepted by the Committee. Punch & Judy men are notoriously vague about dates – after all, why should it matter? – but it's generally accepted he was on the sands from 1926, and a postcard said to be of this date shows the Edmonds' booth.

Could Mr. Beavis have been subletting to him? Was he the drunken showman described by Guy Higgins? It is evident from the Amusement Committee's minutes, which began in 1898, that only

80 Frank Edmonds' first season, 1926.

one booth per season was allowed on the beach. While there may have been the occasional fly-by-nighter, official action would have been taken if two booths were seen there regularly.

Certainly, in the 1930s Frank Edmonds was a fixture on the summer sands, his annual rent reduced to £15 p.a. In 1939 he was given a three-year lease, something of a poor investment, as war broke out that year and the 1940 season was cut short. In September 1940 the 'military authorities' ordered Weymouth Council to clear the beach and sands 'by removal of 390 Beach and stall sites, Vaudeville Pavilion, Bathing machines, Fun Floats'. They were gone for the duration – and many of these attractions did not ever return. In the circumstances, if rather grudgingly, the beach tenants' rents were written off.

In 1944, as soon as the war was seen to be waning, the Committee began their preparations for the 1945 season. Their plans included 'Punch & Judy show as heretofore', plus the donkeys, after their wartime wintering. Frank was offered the pitch at his pre-war rate, and the Committee seemed keen to have him back. By 1947, the beach pitches were 'back in full swing'.

81 Photograph by Revd Tanner of an appreciative audience watching Frank Edmonds in 1926.

In 1949, Mr. J.C.Talbot complained to the Committee about the noise from the 'almost continuous performances' of Punch & Judy on the pitch by King's Statue opposite his offices, which he said made working impossible. The noise was worsened by the introduction of an amplifier, which Frank had turned down at Talbot's request. Despite this gesture, Talbot still wanted the show moved further north.

Members of the Committee visited Talbot's offices to see if his claims were true, and they must have agreed with him, as the booth was moved – immediately provoking a solicitor's letter on behalf of stall-holder Mr. S.H.Mulley, who had rented his King's Statue stall specifically because of the proximity of the Punch & Judy show. Mulley insisted that his trade would be 'seriously reduced' by the booth's removal.

Regardless of this incident – and of competition for the tender from Mr. R.H.Noble of Rochester (who offered £35 against Edmonds' £15) Frank secured the pitch again in 1951. He seems to have been a canny operator, managing to keep his annual rent at £15 for about thirty-five years, despite the best efforts of the Committee to raise it.

1951 was also the year in which there was furious debate about whether the Punch & Judy show should be allowed to take place on a Sunday, a concession Edmonds had requested back in 1946. The vote in a June meeting resulted in a tie, with the Mayor declining to use his casting vote, but in July the matter was agreed, and Frank Edmonds began performing on Sundays. He was limited to the hours between 4pm and 7pm, while Townsend's children's roundabout was allowed from 2.30 to 8.30pm. In 1957, Frank asked if he could extend his Sunday hours. His evening performances must have been competing with some of the many Sunday services being conducted on the beach and Esplanade, by such bodies as the Ebenezer and Bethany Hall, the Salvation Army and St. John's Church. He was told that his request was 'controversial', and debate on the matter was deferred to 1958, but still nothing was agreed. It was not until 1967 that he was allowed to begin performing at 10am on Sundays.

Frank Edmonds died on October 3 1981, only five years after retiring from the beach. His successor was the flamboyant Professor Guy Higgins.

Born on the fifth of November 1933, Guy Higgins's first theatrical experience was – like many children's – a traditional English pantomime. In 2003, he recalled:

> At a very early age I saw traditional pantomimes with girl Principal Boys and very funny, masculine Dames at Worcester's Theatre Royal and the Alexandra. I was inspired by the theatrical ambience... I saw two guest appearances by old-timers, Bransby Williams and Jay Lauriers. The former was a celebrated character actor who portrayed Dickensian characters. He was a musical comedian and I saw his farewell performance as Tweedlepunch in Lesley Stuart's celebrated Flora Dora. I decided this was what I wanted to do and had no doubts I could.

82 Religious meeting on the sands.

As a child, he made model theatres with cardboard characters and painted them. They came 'complete with a replica revolve stage and canvas set design that in the right light looked 3D. From an early age the theatrical thing was everything'.

Guy Higgins's first practical puppet experiences came when he helped out with the Waldo and Muriel Lanchester Marionettes, a much-admired puppet theatre based close to his home in Malvern. By the age of fourteen, he was performing Punch & Judy at garden fêtes and agricultural shows. As a result of all these experiences, the young man wanted to go on the stage as a character actor, but his parents disapproved. Such a career would be uncertain and 'not quite respectable'. Instead, when he left boarding school he was apprenticed to an ecclesiastic and heraldic wood-carver – skills which must have stood him in good stead in his later career. He also joined the Worcester Wizards magic society, of which Alfred Peters of Fernhill Heath, Worcestershire was president. Peters was a retired travelling showman who had worked in music hall and variety, as well as magic. Guy Higgins has described how Peters drove an Austin 16 which was like a double-decker bus, and how he would express himself in 'some very flowery language if the arrangements were not to his liking'. He was doubling as a conjurer and a Punch & Judy man (just as Higgins was to do). The young man helped Peters out in his spare time erecting the booth, hanging up the figures and looking after Dog Toby.

Then, unexpectedly, Alf Peters died, and his widow asked Guy to take over, while refusing to sell her husband's props to him. 'You'll be a better performer if you make your own,' she said. Guy had learnt to make papier-maché and jointed wooden figures at home and also at school in 'a thinly disguised art course', but making booth and props still proved very hard work. His puppets were Mr. Punch, Judy, the Baby, Joey the Clown, the Crocodile, Policeman, Dog Toby (he never had a live dog), the Hangman and a Ghost, with props which included a gallows, a coffin – and a string of sausages. He told the *Malvern Observer* (May 20 1988) 'Canvas for the booth came from a Worcester tentmaker and was brightly striped in red and white. It cost 10/6d. a yard, and I paid three shillings to have it stitched together. I worked all over the Midlands at private and public functions, while still making church furnishings.' He was gaining experience while supplementing his meagre earnings as a woodcarver. 'I was the only Punch & Judy man for miles so there was no shortage of work in the 1950s,' he said.

Thus ended Guy Higgins's apprenticeship. For him, unlike Frank Edmonds, the process had to be learnt rather than absorbed, and Peters' approach must have influenced the way Guy presented his show. Guy went on to be taught by Percy Press senior, who was born in London in 1902 and had worked as a conjurer on Hampstead Heath from Good Friday 1920. There was intense competition for spaces there, and a glut of Punch & Judy shows. Press was to learn how to be a puppeteer some time later, and first performed at the seaside in Swanage in 1935, combining magic and ventriloquism with Punch & Judy. He died in 1980, and is remembered with considerable respect by many Punchmen. Of particular note was his skill in the episode where Punch and Joey count the bodies of Punch's victims, and his timing.

Press passed on his knowledge to Guy, who crammed his days with engagements – with shows, magic and Punch & Judy. Higgins did not give up his day job as an industrial civil servant until 1968. He told the *Echo* about his first appearance on a beach.

> It was a strange experience really. The show was nearly over, there was a good crowd, and the collection box was being handed round. But the tide was coming in quickly. All the time I was looking behind me, I thought that at any moment the booth would be flooded. But I just managed to finish the show with the tide about six feet away from the booth.

Guy spent a season at Tenby before he came to Weymouth and, in his own words, 'never looked back', though the opening season must have been a little unsatisfactory. Weymouth Council had advertised in the *Stage* at short notice and he was booked elsewhere for parts of the summer. He started at Whitsun 1976, doing mostly weekend shows. 'I wouldn't dream of performing on the beaches at Blackpool or Rhyl where long-standing Punchmen have been there for years' he told the *Echo.* 'And I wouldn't have come to Weymouth before Mr. Edmonds retired.' He had visited Weymouth once before for an International Brotherhood of Magicians meeting, but didn't see much of the town on that occasion – 'it rained like heck'. Following his brief appearance in 1976 he was there year upon year for the entire season, beginning at Easter which, on at least one occasion, was snowy.

Guy was soon making innovations to the traditional show. After the Second World War, Frank Edmonds had begun to encourage his audiences to warn Punch when the Ghost or Crocodile sneaked up behind him. This technique, borrowed from music hall, became an accepted part of Punch & Judy performances, and Guy was a master at adroitly involving his audiences. The 'Oh no he didn't! – Oh yes he did!' routine was borrowed from pantomime, and enthusiastically received, especially by children.

Famously, in 1980 Guy introduced a character from the immensely popular American soap opera *Dallas*, a villainous creature called J.R.Ewing who made a 'guest appearance'. Frank Edmonds had ventured a little way in this direction when he changed the name of his boxers. In July 1966 the *Echo* reported that 'Fifteen years ago Frank Edmonds called [his boxers] Sugar Ray Robinson and Randolph Turpin. Seven years ago they were nick-named Floyd Patterson and Ingemar Johannson. Yesterday they were introduced as Henry Cooper and Cassius Clay'. Higgins's J.R., in his ten-gallon hat, featured not just in the local press but in national newspapers and on television too. He caught the imagination as a contemporary bogeyman (just as in his turn Napoleon had done) or as the *Echo* put it, as 'a strong modern symbol of evil and corruption'. During the Second World War, Percy Press had used a Hitler figure for his hangman. Guy liked to have a rogue in his show, rather than a devil. In Victorian times the Devil had to give way to a dragon and then to a Crocodile (borrowed by J.M.Barrie for his *Peter Pan* play, which was first performed in 1904). Though devil and crocodile continue to co-exist, the Crocodile appears more frequently, probably because the Devil has largely lost his power. Punch can be seen confronting his toothy enemy in a photograph of a performance by Professor Smith on Ilfracombe beach in what is probably 1887, since a cameo of Queen Victoria has been added to the proscenium decorations. This Punch is keeping his distance. In Higgins's show, Punch ends by being horribly swallowed – stick and all – by a wide-jawed Croc.

Guy had also included one of the Muppets in his show, and the catch-phrase 'Hi-De-Hi!' from the television series of that name, for which he acted as puppeteer and Punch & Judy adviser. He also appeared in *The Generation Game* and *Jim'll Fix It*. Guy Higgins was always more than ready to move with the times.

Nor was he afraid to change the structure of his show, which could vary quite considerably. He did this often, both in indoor shows and on the beach, by varying the pattern of the action. This had the effect of changing how the audience interpreted the play. A video of some of

83 Punch & Judy dining, by Cruikshank. This looks something of a dangerous domesticity, as both husband and wife are armed.

Higgins's performances over the years included a shot of a list pinned on to the inside wall of his booth, giving the order of appearance for the characters in one of his shows. For example, sometimes the Policeman would appear after Punch had lost the Baby, but before he had assaulted Judy. The Baby is thrown out rather in the same way that a small child would chuck a soft toy out of its pram. He is picked up and put back into the booth, just as the toy would be replaced in the pram, only to be promptly thrown out again. Sometimes, too, the Baby is snapped up by the Crocodile. Punch has been a careless father when this happens, but it's not altogether his fault.

The loss of the Baby seems – within the framework of the show – to be a lesser crime than the attack on poor Judy, who is left lying apparently lifeless on the playboard. (Judy may have started the fight when she belabours Punch with her frying pan, but she has good reason for her anger.) The Policeman usually fails to arrest Punch at this point.

The Punch & Judy Show 185

There's often some affection, of a domestic kind, between Punch and Judy. Punch will mind the Baby while Judy gets the tea. ('We call him Bill, because he came on the first of the month.') After he's hit Judy he says ruefully, 'Judy has a headache – again'. When he is frightened by a Ghost, he calls Judy for consolation. Punch even sings some romantic songs – though to no one in particular, songs such as 'Oh, You Beautiful Doll' and the Victorian 'Lily of Laguna', a favourite of the minstrels.

> *I know she likes me*
> *I know she likes me*
> *Because she says so.*
> *She is my Lily of Laguna,*
> *My lily, and my rose.*

Thus Higgins's Punch is not as bad as he might be – though heartless as they come. And in the end he usually pays the price for his misdeeds.

Like Mark Poulton after him, Guy was interested in the history and origins of Punch & Judy, and his show occasionally made reference to it. As well as incorporating old songs, he used some time-honoured lines, dating back as far as Piccini. When Judy remonstrates with him for losing the baby, he tries to console her by saying that she 'can have another one'. When the Policeman says 'I've come to lock you up,' Punch will retort, 'And I've come to knock you down,' and immediately do so. Guy also added some more recent jokes, in unashamedly music hall style:

> **Policeman**: I'm taking you into apple tart.
> **Punch**: Apple tart?
> **Policeman**: I mean custardy.

There are lots of jokes around the Policeman. He's a country bumpkin – though he is rather unaware of it – slow in speech and

84 *Professor Guy Higgins.*

locomotion. 'We move pretty fast where I come from,' he boasts. Having finally gaoled Punch, he turns his mind to crab sandwiches, cream teas or – in a regular plug – 'a cordon-bleu snack at the Criterion Restaurant'. This is an unwise move: left to his own devices, Punch emerges through the bars like a demented crimson lobster. Once again, he has outwitted the law.

An extract from one of Guy Higgins's shows, published in the *Echo* on August 19 2000, is a characteristic mix of old and new:

> **Punch**: Give us a kiss.
> **Judy**: What – here? In front of all these boys and girls? You'll not get round me like that.
> **Punch**: Oh yes I will.
> **Judy**: Oh no you won't.

Punch: Oh yes I will. (*He grabs her and kisses her violently and noisily.*) There – that's the way to do it.

Judy: You are a rascal Punch. Now I will make you look after the baby. (*She exits.*)

Punch: Oh lovely baby, nice baby, where's the baby, Judy?

Judy: (*Enters with baby and hands to Mr. Punch*) There you are Punch. Now look after him, the little darling. (*To audience*) Now boys and girls, I want you to make sure that Mr. Punch looks after the baby properly. If he doesn't treat it properly will you all call me?

Audience: Yes!

Judy: Very well then. I'll be back Mr. Punch. (*She exits*)

Punch: It's a nice baby. (*He gurgles and croons to the baby then puts it at one end of the playboard and retreats to the opposite side*) Come on baby. Walkee, walkee, walkee. (*Baby toddles across stage. Punch repeats business, baby begins to cry.*) What a cross baby you are. Shut up! (*Baby still cries. Punch bangs baby violently on stage*) Naughty, naughty, naughty baby! (*By now the children should be shouting for Judy. If they are not they can be encouraged by Judy's voice calling, asking if Punch is looking after the baby properly.*)

Punch: Naughty boy, shut up, shut up! (*Baby still cries so Punch bangs it violently on the playboard and throws it out of the booth*) That'll teach it to cry. That's the way to do it. (*Enter Policeman*)

Policeman: Now then, now then, what's going on here?

Punch: (*to audience*) Dixon of Dock Green.

Policeman: Now Mr. Punch, I've a warrant for your arrest.

Punch: You've left your wallet in your vest?

Policeman: I haven't left my wallet in my vest – I've a warrant for your arrest.

Punch: You want a rest?

Policeman: No, I don't want a rest. I've an order to lock you up.

Punch: I've an order to knock you down. (*Does so*)

Policeman: Now then Mr. Punch, striking an officer of the law is a very serious offence. (*He punctuates his remarks with blows from his truncheon, he finally pins Punch against the side of the proscenium*) Can I see your driving licence?

Punch: (*Wriggles free and biffs Policeman*) Here you are then.

Policeman: (*Hits Punch*) Punch, you are a villain.

Punch: So are you. (*Hits him*)

Policeman: That's a good'un.

Punch: That's a better one.

Policeman: That's a topper.

Punch: That's a whopper. (*The fight becomes violent and Punch finally kills the policeman who is put at the end of the playboard.*)

Guy's show was very much his own, often demonstrating a vigorous dislike of bureaucracy and humbug, an anarchic attitude which linked him to Punch's more radical past – though he also enjoyed some aspects of the establishment. He had that mixture of anarchy and conservatism that children have, and this must have been a part of his appeal. He was a fine magician, a member of the Inner Magic Circle with gold star, and also a member of the Grand Order of Water Rats, a fraternity of show business people. He took part in a Children's Royal Variety performance in 1988 and in 2006 attended a Royal Garden Party (to which Mr. Punch, a possible security risk, was not invited).

In summer 2004, Guy Higgins was forced to retire – reluctantly – due to ill-health. He had hoped to continue until he was seventy-five, but this was not to be. His final performance was on September 3 2004. His departure was commemorated at the start of the following season, in a unique ceremony on Tuesday May 17 2005, at his pitch on the beach. Guy was presented with a picture, borough crest and certificate by the Mayor of Weymouth and Portland, Lynne Herbert.

His successor, Mark Poulton, with Punchman Geoff Felix, had made a Professor Guy Higgins puppet for the occasion, which appeared in his special inaugural Punch & Judy show that morning. Guy Higgins had been his inspiration. That morning too, Guy had resprayed the green line on the Esplanade wall, originally drawn, it's thought, by Frank Edmonds. The front of the booth is placed thirty paces seaward from that line, in a tradition which continues. The booth has been in that spot more than in any other place, though it has sometimes been by the Jubilee Clock, or closer to the harbour.

It was Guy's last public appearance on the beach. For almost thirty years he had been a familiar figure on the sands, with his straw boater and his case of puppets. His announcements could be heard from one end of the beach to the other, even as far as the Nothe, where cries of 'That's the way to do it!' once interrupted an official event. Guy died two years later on June 19 2007, and Mark Poulton wrote an

85 *Guy Higgins, with Mark Poulton and tribute puppet, and Mayor Lynne Herbert.*

obituary in which he paid tribute to the man who had been his first inspiration. 'Guy could draw a really huge crowd on the beach and hold them with a slick polished performance and exceptionally clear swazzling.' He ended by quoting Guy's own words, spoken from his booth. 'From here I can generate happiness, and that's what being an entertainer is all about, making people laugh.' This belief shone through every show.

From a very young age, Mark Poulton had wanted to be a Punch & Judy man. He first saw the show in the early 1970s at Weston-super-Mare. The performer was Reuben Staddon (great-grandson of Bert), whose family claimed to have been Punch & Judy men since 1796. Staddon must have put on a fine performance, as the next year when the Poulton family went to Weymouth for their holidays, Mark looked out for a Punch & Judy show, and discovered Guy Higgins. 'I must have watched every performance for that week,' he said. 'I was excited by every show: the noise and voice of Mr. Punch appealed to me. At the end of the holiday I stated that "When I'm grown up, I'm going to be a Punch & Judy man."' He took the stuffing out of his teddy bears to make puppets, dismantled a wall-papering table to use as a booth, and put on a show in the back garden. He continued to perform during his schooldays, and during the Punch & Judy Convention at Covent Garden in 1986 was invited to do some shows with Bill Dane at his seafront pitch in Aberystwyth. He helped out during the summer holidays, and repeated the experience the following year. He found it a tremendous help. Bill Dane, who had a workshop in a converted fire station, taught him how to carve puppets out of lime wood. The scent of lime wood still brings back memories of those days to Mark when he is carving his own puppets. Bill's show, he said, was 'unique'.

The next year – when he was sixteen – Mark won the 'Most Promising Young Prof' award and was asked by Mrs. Anne Codman to do the 1988 season in Llandudno, using their booth. 'This was an honour for me, and although it was a long season I thoroughly enjoyed it,' he said.

Of Romany extraction, the Codmans had been in Llandudno since 1864, when Richard Codman's caravan burnt down there, leaving him stranded. According to Robert Leach, Codman 'already had some knowledge of the Punch & Judy business, and he now collected driftwood from the beach and carved himself a set of figures'. Despite initial opposition from officialdom, the Codman family have been there ever since.

In 1989 Mark left school, passed his driving test and moved to Torquay. This was the start of his professional career. He performed on nearby Goodrington Sands, Paignton, which was a privately-owned beach. 'It was immaculate, no litter, the beach was cleaned every day and there was a good atmosphere.' Unfortunately, the company who owned the beach went into receivership and the Sands were taken over by Torbay Council.

As there was no guarantee of a further contract, Mark began to look elsewhere for work. He consulted Professor Rod Burnett, who had taken over the pitch at Weston after the death of Reuben Staddon. Burnett's show was very different from the Staddon one: it was unscripted and he would pick on the audience. Mark thought it brilliant. Rod Burnett offered Poulton his pitch at Weston for a year and he accepted.

The Weston season was long and busy. It ran from Easter to the end of September, with shows on the hour, every hour. The pitch was a good one – but Mark could only have it for a single summer.

Next he went to Lusty Glaze beach, Newquay. It was now 1991, a wet season, and Mark found that one Cornish beach was not enough to make a living. So he began asking around. Martin Bridle had stopped working his pitch at Broadstairs in Kent and passed it on to Mark. Bridle, who had previously worked two-handed with Rod Burnett in Devon, had a show which derived from Piccini's, but which could also include such characters as a traffic warden, an Arab and Boy George (he was not called Professor Allsorts for nothing). He handed over the pitch to Poulton at the 1992 May Fayre in Covent Garden.

Mark stayed at Broadstairs for the following season as well, leaving the town because the local authority both charged him rent and paid another professor to do shows on the promenade, thus creating an impossible situation. In 1994 he returned to his old pitch at Goodrington Sands, where he stayed until 2003. In 2004 he did a year of private bookings which he disliked, finding them unstimulating and over-regulated. He also did a few days on Paignton's main beach.

When Guy Higgins decided that he would have to retire, he asked Mark to take over for the 2005 season. Poulton moved to Weymouth, where he lived in a caravan for the season. In an interview with the *Echo* that year he told the reporter, 'There's a saying that in a life of Punch & Judy you go from one box to another. Guy did it for twenty-nine years, Frank Edmonds who did it before went from [1926–1976] and I would like to beat both of them, in a nice way.'

Guy Higgins was a constant source of help and advice to Mark Poulton. But, as Mark told the *Echo*, 'we both have very different shows'. An indication of this is their differing attitudes to Mr. Punch. Guy saw his characters as performers, with the potential for making people laugh. He said that sometimes when he was performing, he waited for Punch to say something, and then realised that 'it's me'. When he was being Punch, he felt like Punch, experiencing his anger, his disappointment and his fear. When he was Judy, he experienced Judy's emotions. When Punch hit her over the head, it was as if his own head was being hit. 'I can feel it,' he said. For Mark Poulton, though, they are a medium of expression, like a guitar, say, or any other musical instrument. Like most puppeteers, Mark is attracted to the rebellious and anarchic aspects of Mr. Punch's character, seeing them as an extension of his own personality. The showman makes the puppets, his job is then to make them work for himself.

Although both of these showmen started young, they did not come from Punch & Judy families like Frank Edmonds, who must have known the play as soon as he could talk. They both learnt how to do it by watching other people perform. This method of learning meant they could more easily take liberties with the play. Mark has never

86 Mark Poulton & Mr. Punch unveil the plaque on the Esplanade to Guy Higgins, September 2007.

had a written script; his show is constantly evolving. He stresses the importance of the visual aspects of the show as, without working mouths, puppets have limited means of expression.

On September 3 2007, Mark Poulton and his Mr. Punch unveiled a plaque to Guy Higgins, set in the raised flowerbed on the Esplanade, close to the site of his booth. Professor and puppet were watched by a crowd which included at least five other Punch & Judy men. It was three years to the day since Professor Higgins had performed his last show.

Afterwards, Mark Poulton and Gary Wilson presented an improvised, two-handed show. They paid tribute to Guy Higgins by following the pattern of his show, featuring a particularly agile spider and some of Guy's favourite jokes. But there was a twist in the tale: at the end of the performance two Punch figures were pursued by two crocodiles. This was ingenious and surreal – it was also reassuring. Weymouth, it seems, will never be short of a Mr. Punch.

87 Mark Poulton's booth in the limelight.

Judy

"Judy! Judy! Judy! Judy!" screamed Marret's father from inside his coffin-shaped stage.
"Judy! Judy! Judy! Judy!" There was something unique – like no other sound in the world – about this more than brazen challenge.

John Cowper Powys, *Weymouth Sands*

DESPITE CONTRIBUTING her name to the show, Judy was a latecomer to the party, and one who lacked the distinguished ancestry of a Punch or a Joey. In the Commedia dell'Arte Pulcinella had a wife, while the other *zanni* had only sweethearts. Mr. Punch himself did not always have a wife – a trouble and strife – in the plays, but by 1682 he had found one. She is mentioned in a letter written by Sir Thomas Browne to his daughter-in-law about her nine-year-old-son and his marionette theatre.

He is in great expectation of a tumbler you must send him for his puppet show; a Punch he has and his wife, and a straw king and queen and ladies of honour, and all things but a tumbler…

Mr. Punch had committed himself to matrimony. The name of his wife (when she had one) was Joan, a popular name amongst working people for several centuries. It's been suggested that the name may come from Dame Gigogne, Polichinelle's companion in Paris at the time – 'Gigogne' being anglicised to 'Joan'. Or it may just be an archetypal name for a woman.

Mrs. Punch is pictured in an engraving of 1715, on the stage in Martin Powell's show at Bath. She is a skinny figure beside her humped and rotund husband. In this performance Mr. and Mrs.

88 Judy in Martin Powell's production at Bath.

Punch danced a jig in Noah's Ark, and the play also included a ghost, and a hanging scene. John Payne Collier claimed that these marionettes could move their mouths, which they no doubt put to vigorous use in this medley.

In the early days Joan was usually dressed as a countrywoman, and wore the frilly Georgian mob cap which can still form part of Mrs. Punch's costume. She was younger and more attractive than Judy was to be, and for the practical reasons described elsewhere, less violent in her ways. She developed into more of an Amazon when she became a glove puppet. In Jobson's 'Primitive Puppet Show' at St. Bartholomew Fair in 1790, for example, the climax of the performance is billed as 'a sparring match between those celebrated pugilists Mr. Swatchel (alias Punch) and his wife Joaney'. In earlier days, Mrs. Punch's weapon of choice was a ladle; later it became a frying pan or saucepan.

The earliest reference to 'Judy' (if John Payne Collier's 'Punch's Pranks' is a spoof as seems likely) was in John Keats's review of *Harlequin's Vision* at Drury Lane in 1817–18. Two of the pantomime characters were called 'Punch and Joan', but the poet referred to them as 'Punch and Judy', which Robert Leach has suggested was 'presumably in mistake for what was becoming the commoner name'. (The two names also sound alike when pronounced through a swazzle.) For his part, P.J.Stead suggests that the name, like Toby's, may ultimately derive from the Apocrypha. In the Book of Judith, the eponymous heroine chops off the head of Holofernes, her people's Assyrian enemy. *Judith and Holofernes* was a popular fairground drama, so the story would have been well-known. Joan, too, was a name which had fallen out of fashion, being replaced by 'Jane'.

But Judy was also a name for a tramp's woman in nineteenth-century slang, a period when the puppet became coarser as well as more violent. When she makes her entry in Collier's version of the play, she slaps Punch's face the moment he tries to kiss her. (Judy: 'Take that then: how do you like my kisses? Will you have another?' and all before Punch has merited such treatment.) Shrewish Judy has aged considerably with her change of name. In Cruikshank's illustrations she looks more like a grandmother than the mother she has become in the nineteenth century, when the Baby begins to make his brief and fatal appearances. (There had been references to Punch's children before this, but they did not appear on stage.)

Judy's Ghost often featured in the nineteenth century, when she returned to haunt her murderer. This happens in the play described to Mayhew by the Punch & Judy man in the 1850s. He explained:

> The Ghost represents the ghost of Judy, because he's killed his wife, don't you see, the Ghost making her appearance; but Punch don't know it at the moment. Still he sits down tired, and sings in the corner of the frame the song of 'Home, sweet Home,' while the Sperrit appears to him.
>
> Punch turns round and sees the Ghost, and is most terribly timidated. He begins to shiver and shake in great fear, bringing his guilty conscience to his mind of what he's been guilty of doing, and at last he falls down in a fit of frenzy.

Kicking, screeching, hollaring, and shouting 'Fifty thousand pounds for a doctor!' Then he turns on his side and draws hisself double with the screwmatics in his gills.

Such melodrama was a Victorian speciality; ghosts are scarcer today, they have faded in the bright light of modern scepticism. Should one appear in a contemporary show, it's more of a frightener than a revenant, and Punch displays little remorse or repentance for his actions. He just wants the Ghost to go away.

Mayhew's Punchman told him that although Piccini brought Punch into the streets of England, he was not the pioneer. 'To be sure, there was a woman over with it before then. Her name was – I can't think of it just now, but she never performed in the streets...' If this mystery woman ever existed she would have been a rare creature. Even today, Punch & Judy puppeteers are overwhelmingly male. After all, it's something of a male show, with Judy as the sole female puppet.

89 *Judy handing the baby to Punch, by Cruikshank.*

Yet a woman puppeteer has performed in Dorset – at Swanage, to the east of Weymouth. Guy Higgins's mentor, Percy Press, had a pitch there in 1935; other showmen included Ernie Brisbane and Jock Armitage (with his swazzle incorporated into his dental plate). Then in the late 1970s, the little seaside town saw its first ever female puppeteer, Wendy Wharam.

Wendy Wharam was Swanage's Punch & Judy professor for about eighteen years. A puppeteer who was working in the theatre, she had been researching the show and soon became involved with the characters, especially Punch, whose anarchic, anti-authority attitude drew her to him. So, when the regular (if short-lived) Punch & Judy man left Swanage beach, she took over the pitch.

As well as the beach show, Wendy was doing another Punch & Judy show next to the Arnolfini Gallery in Bristol. Since it struck her as odd that she as a feminist should be presenting such a play she began doing a Judy & Punch show instead. As she had no one to bottle for her then, she made Judy tease Punch, accusing him of having 'a woman under your skirt!' Judy encouraged the audience to shout 'Come on out!' and Wendy emerged to collect the money.

Mocked as he was, Punch still 'wouldn't lie down'. He was not just a misogynist, he was a trickster too in the old tradition, and a survivor. Punch was the sort of character you love to hate, a good foil for the other characters. He was, she said, 'an ass, arrogant like a lot of men we know'. Wendy found it great fun to play around with his character. She felt that you could not help but be slightly fond of him. There was a kind of bond between them, especially after all the time she spent making him perform. She said it was 'the anarchist in me' which empathised with Punch.

Her Judy puppet was a feisty character too, who gave as good as she got. Punch was in fact quite a hen-pecked creature in the show. Despite her baby, Judy was an elderly character, and with her large hooked nose she was certainly no beauty. Judy usually commanded the sympathy of the crowd, though they would become rather more torn when her husband was made to look foolish, which swayed their sympathies towards him.

One of Wendy's characters was her own invention. Made from a piece of fur, he was called Fleasy, and was loved by the children in the audience. As flea-ridden as his name suggests, he was always scratching himself. Fleasy had boot-button eyes and a furry tail. The tail came from his mother, who was a squirrel, while his father was that most infested of animals, a hedgehog.

Wendy had no script. Like most professors, she used some of the old jokes which had been handed down as well as some of her own. As an example, she told the joke about Judy asking Punch to babysit – whereupon he obligingly sits on the baby. Such a visual pun is highly suitable for using with glove puppets.

She also exploited the fact that while she could see her audiences, they could not see her. If a little boy started throwing sand, the policeman would pop up on to the playboard and threaten to book him for his crime. Embarrassed, the child would realise that he had been found out and stop immediately. This sort of approach involved the audience more directly than any 'Oh yes you did!' routine.

On Swanage beach Wendy's bottler was Peter Jaggard. She taught him to do the show and then they took it in turns to perform. Peter has continued with the show since Wendy 'retired' ten years ago. He has two very keen and talented apprentices helping him, so with luck the tradition will be carried on by these young performers.

Wendy added that she liked the fact that Punch & Judy is such an egalitarian show. Broad-based, the show attracts old and young, rich and poor. It is the last of the street theatres. The living is of course precarious – if it rains you don't earn anything – and yet it's worth it. Wendy said she felt quite restless in the spring, like a swallow, when the season was approaching – and reluctant to leave at the end of the summer when the show was finally over.

As Wendy Wharam's experiences have revealed, it requires a fair amount of ingenuity to perform a show (unless it's a contracted one) without someone to collect the money.

90 Wendy Wharam in front of her Swanage booth, with Fleasy.

For many years, Frank Edmonds' father-in-law bottled for him: it was always wise to keep the money-collecting in the family. Michael Byrom suggests that the word 'bottler' is probably a corruption of the French *bateleur*, which could mean 'a charlatan, a mountebank, a strolling player'. Since a bottle was actually used, the origin of the word may be plainer. Any money dropped into the bottle would be difficult to get out inconspicuously: but it was still wise to be watchful. If one of the family was not available, then Frank advised that 'a bottler who has only one arm is preferred – but if he has two arms, the traditional joke says that you should catch a fly and make him hold it in his spare hand: if he still has the fly at the end of the show, the collection will be all right'. When Frank travelled around as a young man, he would be accompanied by his bottler, with whom he split the takings. 'I always reckoned a good outside man was worth as much as a good inside man,' he said.

The bottler used to wear a top hat and carry the traditional pipe and drum. He would play tunes such as 'We were Sweethearts' and 'In the Shade of the Old Apple Tree' to attract the crowd. Before the performance, he would converse with the offstage Mr. Punch, cajoling him to make an appearance. Other tasks were to give clues, such as 'Judy, you're wanted' to the puppeteer at crucial points during the performance, and to encourage audience participation.

Rene Smith works as a bottler. She has been Professor Mark Poulton's bottler on Weymouth beach since he set up his booth there in 2005. Before that, she was Guy Higgins's bottler for almost the whole of his turn as Weymouth's Punch & Judy man.

Edmonds, Higgins, Poulton all 'busked' for a living – as their predecessors had done. They are not paid, they rely on what the bottler collects, and this collection can be hard work. Rene listed some of the excuses members of the audience gave for not paying up. They have no change, they are only stopping for a moment – or, more bizarrely, they are waiting for a bus. Anything rather than pay the modest sum requested for watching the show.

Before she became a bottler, Rene had worked in the brewery trade, running two pubs and then an off-licence on Abbotsbury Road in Weymouth. Guy Higgins lived in a caravan off that road and behind the circus. He used to pop into the shop to change his cash into notes and sometimes to buy whisky. Since Rene never went on the beach (and had never seen a Punch & Judy show even when she was a child in Blackpool, a resort which abounded in them) these were the only occasions on which they met.

Then Guy advertised for a pensioner to bottle for him. Noticing the advertisement, Rene decided to reply, as a joke. 'Do I know you?' he asked her at the interview. He first offered the job to an actual pensioner, who turned it down. So Rene got the job, unpaid. 'You don't get paid until you get your pension,' Guy joked. He used to pay her in cream teas – they would try out different places each afternoon. She became very friendly with Guy and his wife Maggie. Rene has boxes of photographs of life on the beach, meeting entertainers such as Ken Dodd and Paul Daniels who were appearing in the summer season at the Pavilion, going for outings, playing tricks (once when Rene was up a ladder helping to assemble the booth, Guy sneaked inside and attacked her with the Crocodile). There could be wilder beasts around as well. In August 1988, when the circus still used live animals, the trainer would wash his elephants in the sea. Rene was innocently

91 *Circus elephants in the sea at Weymouth, by Rene Smith.*

paddling in the shallows beside them when they turned and charged her. She had the presence of mind to take a photograph before she ran.

Like many showmen, Guy Higgins also did private bookings, including on a number of *champêtre* and Venetian evenings at Stourhead. On their way to Wiltshire once, Guy and Rene stopped for tea. Rene was asked, 'Are you the lady with the straw hat?' She had been recognised from Weymouth beach. Much to their mutual amusement, the Punch & Judy man, who spent most of his time hidden in his booth, went totally unnoticed.

In 1986 there was a Royal Variety Show at the Pavilion in front of Prince Andrew and Sarah Ferguson. Guy was invited to appear, and Rene acted for the night as his dresser. Guy was all in white and blacked up, in the style of one of his music hall heroes, G.H.Elliott, who called himself the 'famous chocolate-coloured coon'. Guy told the *Western Gazette* in 2003 'I got to know him by visiting his dressing-room and ended up having cups of tea. His showmanship, stage presence, the way he handled the audience – everyone felt included –

92 *Rene Smith waiting to catch the baby in a performance at the Dorchester show.*

and his soft-shoe shuffle made him an idol. I got permission from his wife to follow in his steps after he'd gone. I learnt the soft-shoe shuffle and did some of his engagements'.

To survive financially, a Punch & Judy man has to be versatile – and so, it seems, does his bottler.

Other female voices than Judy's have been raised on the beach. Some of these were suffragettes, members of the National Union of Women's Suffrage Society, the non-militant wing of the female emancipation movement, who held meetings on the sands at Whitsuntide in 1914.

In February of the previous year, the Conservative & Unionist Women's Franchise Association had held a public meeting at the Hotel Burdon (now the Prince Regent). The speakers were Lady Betty Balfour and Laurence Housman, both of whom had more eminent siblings: Balfour's sister was the noted suffragist Lady Constance Lytton, while Laurence's brother was the poet A.E.Housman.

The meeting was both peaceful and effective. But by May the *Southern Times* was reporting that Housman had since faced 'a wild, infuriated mob in Hyde Park' where he was forced 'to beat a hasty retreat'. This incident so alarmed the newspaper that they predicted a summer of copycat militant action in Weymouth.

> Information furnished to the police is to the effect that the 'wild women' are now expected to turn their unwelcome attention to prospective holiday makers, in view of the near approach of the holiday season. Vacant houses at the seaside, country cottages, concert rooms, band stands, piers, and other buildings associated with the holiday season are likely to be burned down or otherwise destroyed as occasion presents itself. The unoccupied town houses of persons on holiday will also be the object of incendiary plots.

Despite the attack on his person, Laurence Housman continued to stay loyal to the cause. On being called to jury service a month later, he said in court, 'I cannot conscientiously be a party to trying women while they are not on an equal footing with men, and therefore I ask your lordship to excuse me.'

There was no arson reported in Weymouth – or anywhere else in Dorset – that summer. Perhaps because of this fact, the National Union was allowed to hold a camp from May 30 to June 6 1914. The camp, the first of its kind in the country, was pitched below Southdown Farm, between a plantation and Lodmoor, on a site which offered the merest glimpse of the sea. It contained about sixty women, who came mostly from the south-west of the country. The camp comprised a large dining tent, a library tent, an enquiry office, a kitchen and the members' tents. Discipline was strict: with regular hours and a special uniform of 'green coat and skirt with a white shirt blouse and a tie of the Union's rainbow colours, and a green felt hat turned up at the side. Jewellery, tight skirts and fancy blouses are considered out of place', reported the *Southern Times*.

The intention was to train the women as campaigners (and campers) and also as 'missionaries'. 'The members sally forth in the neighbouring villages, with one special object in view, that being to arrest the baleful influences which militancy has been wholly responsible for.'

The women had their own newspaper, 'West Country Campers', with a map and details of events around Weymouth. There was a full programme at the camp as well, including an Entertainment Night on Thursday, June 4th when Walter Raymond (author of *Gentleman Upcott's Daughter* and lecturer on folklore), recited some popular verses from the work of William Barnes, 'the Dorsetshire poet'.

To advertise the entertainment, sandwich board women paraded up and down the Esplanade. As even sandwich board men were rare outside London, the suffragettes must have attracted a good deal of attention.

The daily beach meetings also drew the crowds. The Union had applied for permission for these events from the Borough's Amusement Committee who, probably expecting trouble, stipulated that their consent was subject to 'position being allotted by the Chief Constable, and their making arrangements for the necessary police protection'.

The week seems to have been remarkably successful, and was favourably reported by the local *Southern Times*. But the year was 1914; war broke out in August – and nothing more was heard of these activities, like many others on the sands.

93 Suffragettes on Weymouth Esplanade, 1914.

Encore 1:
The Theatre Royal

THE REDISCOVERY OF the room which was once the auditorium of the Theatre Royal – an interior often graced by the presence of a king and his court – has attracted surprisingly little attention in Weymouth. More effort seems to have gone into discrediting the find than to exploring its possibilities.

In *Recollections of a Nonagenerian* (1914) James Eaton Robens described the old theatre as 'a most curious little place [which] lay at the back of a confectioner's shop, No.10 Augusta Place, the width being the same as that of the small assembly room behind the present restaurant, but of greater depth... The fortunes of the place got very low; at last it was closed for months at a time, when one winter night, about 1849, an alarm of fire was raised. Fortunately there was no wind, and before the fire reached the masses of old scenery stored beneath the stage it was extinguished'. (Robens goes on to speculate whether or not the fire was deliberate. If so, the arsonist was targeting old and unusual buildings. The ice house on Greenhill Terrace was destroyed around the same time.) Robens added that 'The theatre was still used as such for several years after the fire, but it was such an out-of-date place that when the front house was re-built the whole premises were altered, and a small assembly room now occupies the greater part of the site.' (Robens was wrong here, the back room still has the same dimensions as the old theatre.)

After it was closed in 1859, the theatre did indeed become an eating-house or restaurant. According to the *Weymouth Visitors' List* for 1863 the commercial occupier was 'Howe Confectioner' (a Mrs. and a Miss Bowman were also listed as living at No. 10). *Braizer's Register* of 1868 contains an advertisement for Howe's Refreshment Rooms, premises which offer 'chops, steaks, soups, entrées. Public & Wedding Breakfasts. Dinners, Rout [a large party or social gathering] & Ball. Suppers Completely Furnished. Choice Wines.'

If Howe lived up to his grand claims, then he must have been using a large part of the building – probably the ground and first floors. The second floor would then be given over to tenants who were most likely visitors.

'William Howe, confectioner' was still there (and advertising) in 1875 according to the directories, after which another confectioner, Henry Cooke, is listed for 1880,1885 and 1889. In addition, by 1895 Henry Cooke was also trading from 2 Bond Street, which had been the side entrance to the theatre – suggesting that the rear of the building at least had been little changed. Cooke was still there in 1898, but no occupier is given by *Kelly's Directory* for 1903. This may have been because building works were in progress. A missing document of 1902 in Dorset History Centre's catalogue is described as being 'plans and

Telephone 0467 (3 minutes from Station, 1 minute from Pier),
Telegrams—"Thompson, Weymouth."

The Weymouth Hotel
and Restaurant, ───

COMMERCIAL AND PRIVATE.

Facing the ENGLISH NAPLES BAY.

ACCOMMODATION FOR PARTY OF 200
AND PRIVATE ROOMS FOR 50.

Special Terms for Commercials.

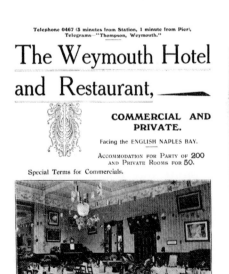

SPECIAL 2/- COURSE LUNCHEONS.
Do.   1/6   do.   do.

BREAKFASTS, LUNCHEONS, DINNERS, TEAS, AND SUPPERS,—As per Menu—at any time.

SPECIALITY: Dinners from Joint and two Vegetables, **1/-**

FULLY LICENSED.

All Wines, Spirits & Ales,   From the best-known Brewers and Distillers, at popular Prices.

Head Quarters of the Weymouth Angling Society.

Proprietor— **J. W. THOMPSON**
(FROM LONDON)

94 J.W.Thompson's advertisement for the Weymouth Hotel, c.1904.

sections of restaurant in Augusta Place for Sir F.J.W.Johnstone Bart'. By 1904, J.W.Thompson ('from London') had opened the Weymouth Hotel and Restaurant. The *Visitors' Free Guide to Sunny Weymouth* of that year boasts of Thompson's 'London prices' (surely a dubious recommendation?) and of a 'Large Hall to accommodate 200 people'.

In another of Thompson's advertisements, the first floor window of No.10 can just be seen, looking much the same as it does today. It seems likely that as a part of the alterations, the (already much-altered) remains of the original frontage were replaced by a façade which Eric Ricketts described as 'high gabled and in the romantic vein of the late 19th century'. It's a handsome and striking façade, its height boosted by an extra floor, and it stands out among the Georgian frontages of the Esplanade with which it once discreetly blended.

If Johnstone was responsible for the change, then the front of the building is Edwardian rather than Victorian. An engraving of 1842 and a Frith photograph of the 1890s picture the row without this lofty incomer – though with a third storey acquired at some time between the two illustrations – while in a photograph of 1923 the new frontage is in place. Each storey had two sets of bay windows, each set merged into one in the alterations.

In 1907 Charles Henry Ship was the proprietor of the establishment which was by now advertised as being at 10 Augusta Place and 4 Upper Bond Street. Ship published a plush (if undated) souvenir brochure for his

95 The Edwardian frontage to 10 Augusta Place in 2007.

establishment, informing the reader that the building has been 'entirely reconstructed'. A photograph of the ground-floor frontage has (as well as a reclining dog) oriel windows, a pair of elaborate lamps and some stained glass, all snug between 'The Cosy' café at number 9 and the business at number 11, a dwelling used by hair-dressers since at least 1898.

Inside are Saloon and Buffet Bars, well-stocked and gleaming. On the first floor – immediately over the bars – 'a large, handsome, and delightful Tea and Dining Room', gives fine views of the coast. To the rear on the first floor is the building's glory, the Dining Hall, which was also used as a ballroom and for concerts.

> Situate within easy access from the Hotel, it is some 40 feet square with a high and well ventilated glass roof, the walls being made attractive by handsome paintings and other pictures, and the windows draped with much taste and artistic skill. The Hall will accommodate about 150 persons at dinner, and is often patronised by large excursion parties in the summer season. It possesses, too, some Historic interest, as it occupies the site of the Old Theatre Royal, which King George III, frequently patronised, and where on several occasions during his long residence in Weymouth, His Majesty caused the news of British Victories to be announced from the Stage. It is acknowledged to be the finest Dancing Room in Dorset, and is extensively patronised by devotees of the Terpsichorean Art. The Hall is illuminated both with Gas and Electric Light. The Bijou Band is in attendance from 8 to 11p.m. in the summer season. The approach is by a fine broad staircase from the Bond Street entrance.

The size of the Dining Hall, it should be noted, is the same as that of the old theatre, and since the brochure is at pains to point out the 'easy access', this must be from theatre's Bond Street entrance. Mr. Ship is making the most of the room's history, realising its value.

96 Side entrance to the Theatre Royal in Bond Street, adjoining the side entrance to the Weymouth Hotel bars.

A photograph in the brochure shows the Dining Hall, with separate tables and waitresses poised for service. The windows which look on to New Street at the rear can be seen with the stencilled eyelids they still retain.

The room does not seem to have been altered by Ship or his predecessor. It has a high glass skylight, which means that extra floors were added only on to the front. (These houses had distinct front and back sections.) In fact the changes seem to have mainly affected the front of the building both on the Esplanade and at No 4 Bond Street, where a side entrance to the bars is still distinguishable. (Faint traces of the words 'The Weymouth Restaurant' can be deciphered.)

It would after all be difficult to demolish a room embedded in a terrace of houses without affecting 9 Augusta Place to the south and the properties in Bond Street to the north – and also number 11, since the auditorium reaches across the rear part of its first floor.

The auditorium is a high-quality space; there is nothing else like it anywhere in the Borough. The ceiling beam pattern of rectangular panels was a design used up to the end of the seventeenth century, which continued to be copied. and the acanthus leaves in the cornices were a classical motif from the late seventeenth and eighteenth centuries. Plasterwork expert Jane Penoyre has dated the ceiling work to around the late eighteenth century, which was the period when the theatre began. In addition, there is the well-restored frieze, which can also be seen as it was a century ago, in the Dining Hall section of Ship's hotel brochure. It is a delicate and delightful tracery of floral swags, small putti-figures and musical instruments, a design typical of the late seventeenth and early-eighteenth centuries.

At some point during the twentieth century, frieze and beams were covered up, and only came to light again when the false ceiling was removed in 2002. They are a remarkable survival. Many Georgian theatres have been lost, while Weymouth's royal theatre, which is of national (if not European) importance, has made a dramatic reappearance.

Encore 2:
Puppets on the Move

Here a knave in a fool's coat, with a trumpet sounding or a drum beating, invites you to see his puppets. Here a rogue like a wild woodman, or in an antic shape like an incubus, desires your company to view his motion.

From an old pamphlet, quoted by Walter Wilkinson in *Vagabonds and Puppets*

BETWEEN THE FIRST and the Second World Wars, English puppetry underwent a revival as an art form. One of the best known puppeteers to emerge from this movement was Walter Wilkinson. Born and brought up in Letchworth, Wilkinson and his brother Arthur toured England in a caravan, performing with hand-carved marionettes. Arthur continued to make marionettes which, after he married Lily Gair, were called the Gair Wilkinson Marionettes. Walter meanwhile began to create glove puppets. As a travelling showman, he wandered with them through England, Scotland, Wales and America.

Although usually mistaken for Punch & Judy figures, Wilkinson's puppets were his own invention – his Peep Show – using characters such as John Barleycorn, Uncle Joe the boxer and Mickey the Monkey. Punch, not normally noted for his tact or flexibility, is his 'stage-manager'. Of the conventional Punch & Judy figures, Wilkinson wrote in 1927 that 'it is very easy to frighten children by throwing the baby out of the window, by the murders, the gruesome hanging, and the stuffing of a corpse into a black coffin … after three hundred years we might try to think of something a little more suitable to the times.'

97 Three of Walter Wilkinson's puppets.

By 1944 he seemed to have changed his mind, publishing an article which told how much he had enjoyed such gory details when he first encountered the show as a child.

> Crossing the market place, lost in some childish imagination, I found myself entangled in a small, loose crowd, and became aware of a queer strident voice piercing the air. Looking up I was astonished to see over the heads of the crowd a sort of gaudily painted frame with a little live man in it – a fantastic, rather terrifying old man, about twelve inches high, who was bashing the gaudy frame with a thick, dirty stick which he hugged to his body. Something stirred in my little diaphragm; excitement welled up in my inside and I let out a sudden hoot of delight and rapture that made the crowd turn and look at me... I doubt if I knew that this was a Punch & Judy show. It must have been my first taste of costumed drama – the fantastic, highly-coloured life of the stage. I fell for it at once.

With his new-style puppets, Wilkinson took to the road, travelling on foot from place to place with his frame, his tent, his Willesden green canvas bucket (a much-admired luxury) and his Primus stove. He braved the wind on the heath, the rain on the plain and the cold, cold snow. His tent caught fire, his clothes were often soaked, but on he walked, describing his adventures as he went, in a series of once very popular books.

Like any puppeteer, he had to seek permission to perform. Frank Edmonds described the routine, which he had learnt from his father, to Robert Leach.

> The routine followed when he and his bottler arrived in a village involved, first, a visit to the Police Station, then to the school, where permission was requested to entertain the children after school. They would pay a penny or twopence, and at the end were told to tell anyone they knew that there would be another performance later on the village green or outside the pub.

Walking was the way to do it for Wilkinson. He hated cars, which were then in their very early stages of destroying the countryside. He was, he wrote, that 'wandering anachronism, a pedestrian on a main road of the twentieth century'. A chapter in his book *Vagabonds and Puppets* (1930) records an anticipatory form of road rage:

> All the motor-cars of the country seemed to be rushing on the Sandy City. Every moment one more flashed by, and the chauffeurs, glorying in their craft, seemed to pass on the narrowest margin. The wind from the great cars staggered me; the rattle of the fiery, mechanical stream flayed my nerves, and I was roused into a great temper, and then – I began to enjoy myself. There piled up inside me an immense contempt for the poor silly fools who, sealed up in leather

and enclosed in glass and metal cases, were rushed away by their silly engines from all that was lovely, exquisite and life-giving in the sunny day.

The 'Sandy City' of this passage is Bournemouth, another pet hate, along with Oxford, London and most other cities (with the single exception of Bath). He was dubious too about the railways, complaining about the discomforts of train travel. Wilkinson disliked the modern world, he was searching for the simple life of an imagined past. He envied the old roadmender his years of stone-breaking, and admired the sentiments of his hostess at a tea party (one of many social functions to which he managed to wangle an invitation). This lady was a school-teacher who regarded the education of children as an unnecessary process. The girls would naturally become servants, and the boys would be farm workers. So why bother with books?

Though not above some mild self-mockery, Wilkinson was a person of decided opinions, many of which derived from his upbringing in Letchworth, his own birthplace and that of the Garden City movement. The place attracted many of the cranks of the day – smocked and sandalled Arts & Crafts types. The first public house to open in Letchworth was the Skittles Inn (1907), which served only ginger beer and lemonade. Even Wilkinson drew the line at this. He wrote:

Now what did they want with a milk-and-water pub
When milk shops they were rich in?
Come on, boss! Let's go and have a drink!
We can get one down in 'itchin.

In his wide wanderings Wilkinson scarcely touched on Dorset. Apart from his reluctant (though profitable) 'flirt' with the Sandy City (then in Hampshire) he made a brief, disappointing foray into Wimborne, where the 'rural slaves' were too oppressed to offer him a site to stay for the night. His travels, recorded in his many books, still have a certain period charm, that of the journals (not without shrewdness) of a gentleman puppeteer. Some of his experiences were similar to those of any other showman and provide valuable information about their travelling lives. While working his way through Somerset and North Devon in his first book *The Peep Show* (1927), he visits the late Professor Smith's pitch at Ilfracombe, meets the late Professor Hill of Bath's 'nobber' and is accosted by a member of the Staddon family. Unfortunately, nowhere in his more south-easterly journeyings in *Vagabonds and Puppets* does Wilkinson come across a traditional Punch & Judy man – a Maggs or an Edmonds. It would have made an interesting encounter.

Walter Wilkinson was not without followers, inspired by his books. In 1931, three Weymouth women, Marie Hownam Meek of Rodwell, Christiana Falkner (niece of John Meade Falkner) and Ruth Halls formed the Moonstruck Marionettes. They toured the county and beyond in a series of temperamental cars. Their first car, a Baby Austin, was nicknamed the Duckling and did not last long under its load of puppeteers, puppets and scenery. The Duckling was succeeded by Boniface and Alexander, two cars being a great, if unreliable, luxury.

The women used marionettes rather than glove puppets: they had moved even further than Walter Wilkinson from the traditional Punch & Judy show. Their characters were taken high-mindedly from folk-tales and Scottish ballads, although they did include a brace of boxers and a clown. Their travelling lives were modelled on Wilkinson's (who would not have approved of motorised vehicles, however endearingly named).

Their adventures are recorded in three handwritten volumes, entitled *A Short History of an Amusing Enterprise: the Moonstruck Marionettes*, illustrated with box-camera photographs. The existing copy is a rewritten replacement of the original, which was destroyed by an incendiary bomb in 1941. Impressionistic, jokey, the history provides an entertaining picture of the village halls, mansions and private houses in which they performed. (Another venue was the Cerne Abbas workhouse.) Most of their performances were in Dorset, but the intrepid trio motored as far as Sheffield, South Wales, Cheltenham Ladies' College –

and a house in London's Leicester Square. As well as the erratic nature of their transport, there were other hazards, such as heath fires, and an unexpected firing-range where shooting was in progress.

In 1934 Ruth Halls left the puppeteers to get married (to one of John Meade Falkner's nephews). She was replaced by Grace Wadsworth, and the show went on – until the kill-joy Second World War put an end to the enterprise. It may have been a long way from Punch & Judy, but it had something of the same wandering and independent spirit.

98 The three puppeteers. From the left: Christiana Falkner, Mrs Hownam Meek and Grace Wadsworth, 1935

Curtain

'Ah! *Vanitas Vanitatum!* Which of us is happy in this world? Which of us has his desire? Or, having it, is satisfied? – Come children, let us shut up the box and the puppets, for our play is played out.'

William Makepeace Thackeray, *Vanity Fair*

What a pity! What a pity!

Mr. Punch

Bibliography

SINCE MUCH OF THIS BOOK is about the Punch & Judy show, it should be noted that no two commentators entirely agree on the origins of the play or its development. Some writers place more importance on the pre-Commedia period in Italy than others. I tend to agree with Philip John Stead, who remarks that no connection can be proved, as there is no continuity. (He adds that 'things are not "descended", they recur'.) For Stead, too, the Punches of the various countries are 'akin', but take on their own national characteristics.

George Speaight, in his seminal *History of the English Puppet Theatre* (1955) claimed that 'there is a clear case for claiming a purely English origin for Punch & Judy'. While Punch had come over from Italy to England in 1662 as Pulcinella, the other characters derived from English folk drama.

For his part, Michael Byrom (a Punch & Judy man at Brighton and Paignton) took an opposing view, stressing the Italian origins of the show, which he claimed was brought over to England almost in its entirety by Giovanni Piccini. Byrom also suggests that Piccini probably came to England via Paris, as Punch, his booth, and most of the characters were closer to the French show than to the Italian one – a view endorsed by John Payne Collier.

Speaight modified his views in later years, when evidence came to light that the Italians had used live dogs in the show from 1760 at the latest, and that such features as Punch tricking the Hangman, and the quarrel over the ownership of Toby, were traditional in Italy.

More recently, Robert Leach in his *Punch & Judy Show* (1985) pays tribute to Speaight's 'spadework' in his *History of the English Puppet Theatre*. Leach, to whom I am indebted, describes the performances of many Punch & Judy professors. I have followed this lead, homing in on the Weymouth performers, about whom most information is oral.

THE MAIN BIBLIOGRAPHICAL SOURCES I have used for **Punch & Judy** are listed below:

Byrom, Michael. *Punch & Judy its origin and evolution*, Norwich, DaSilva Puppet Books, revised edition 1988

Byrom, Michael. *Punch in the Italian Puppet Theatre*, London, Centaur Press,1988

Leach, Robert. *The Punch & Judy Show, History, Tradition and Meaning*, London, Batsford, 1985 (LEACH)

Speaight, George. *The History of the English Puppet Theatre*, Carbondale and Edwardsville, Southern Illinois University Press, second edition 1990 (SPEAIGHT 1)

Speaight, George. *Punch & Judy, a history*, London, Studio Vista, revised edition 1970 (SPEAIGHT 2)

Stead, Philip John. *Mr. Punch*, London, Evans Brothers, 1950

And for Weymouth:

Attwooll, Maureen. *The Bumper Book of Weymouth*, Tiverton, Halsgrove, 2006 (ATTWOOLL 1)

Boddy, Maureen & West, Jack. *Weymouth an Illustrated History*, Wimborne, Dovecote Press, 1983 (ATTWOOLL 2)

Boddy, Maureen & West, Jack. *Seaside Weymouth A Celebration in Pictures*, Wimborne, Dovecote Press, 1989

Pritchard, Geoff and Hutchins, Andy. *Weymouth and Portland*, Stroud, Tempus, 2004

Staelens, Yvonne. *Weymouth Through Old Photographs*, Exeter, Dorset Books, 1989

CHAPTER ONE

Published sources

ATTWOOLL 2, *op. cit.*

Collier, John Payne (ed.). *Punch & Judy with Illustrations*, London, S.Prowett, second edition (including preface and notes)1828

George, David J. & Gossip, Christopher J. *Studies in the Commedia dell'Arte*, Cardiff, University of Wales Press, 1993

Good, Ronald. *Weyland*, Dorchester, Longmans, 1945

Graves, Richard Perceval. *The Brothers Powys*, London, Routledge & Kegan Paul, 1983

Krissdóttir, Morine. *John Cowper Powys and the Magical Quest*, London, Macdonald, 1980

Krissdóttir, Morine (ed.). *Petrushka and the Dancer. The Diaries of John Cowper Powys 1929–1939*, Manchester, Carcanet Press, 1995

Powys, John Cowper. *Autobiography*, New York, Simon & Schuster, 1934

Powys, John Cowper. *A Glastonbury Romance*, New York, Simon & Schuster, 1932

Powys, John Cowper. *Jobber Skald*, London, Bodley Head, 1935

Powys, John Cowper. *Letters to his Brother Llewelyn*, London, Village Press, 1975

Powys, John Cowper. *Weymouth Sands*, New York, Simon & Schuster, 1934

Powys, John Cowper. *Wolf Solent*, New York, Simon & Schuster, 1929

Powys, Llewelyn. *Dorset Essays*, London, Bodley Head, 1935

Powys, Llewelyn. *Letters of Llewelyn Powys*, London, Bodley Head, 1943

Rudlin, John. *Commedia dell'Arte an Actor's Handbook*, London, Routledge, 1994

Stevenson, Robert Louis. *A Child's Garden of Verses*, London, Longmans,1885

Waite, A.E. *Key to the Tarot*, London, Rider, new edition 1972

Woolf, Virginia, *Mrs. Dalloway*, London, Hogarth Press, 1925

Dorset Yearbook 1960-61
Moran, Margaret, 'The Vision and Revision of John Cowper Powys's *Weymouth Sands.*' *Powys Review* 11, 1982/83
Pashka, Linda, 'Powys's Punch & Judy Shows: *Weymouth Sands* and Misogyny', *Powys Notes*, Spring 1990
Powys, John Cowper, ' "Remembrances": *Weymouth Sands*', *Powys Review* 11, 1982/83

Unpublished sources

Falkner, John Meade. 'Notes by John Meade Falkner 1859–71' (1925), Dorset History Centre: D300/12
Powys, Llewelyn. 'Lodmoor', typescript in the possession of the author
Recollections of Sheila Milton. Conversations with Maureen Attwooll and Richard Samways

CHAPTER TWO

Published sources

Brown, Frederick. *Theater and Revolution*, New York, Viking Press, 1980
Carné, Marcel. *Les Enfants du Paradis*, London, Lorrimer, 1968
Dick, Kay. *Pierrot*, London, Hutchinson, 1960
Hartnoll, Phyllis (ed.) *The Oxford Companion to the Theatre*, Oxford, Oxford University Press, 1972
Holmes, Richard, *Sidetracks*, London, HarperCollins, 2000
Lee, Hermione. *Virginia Woolf*, London, Chatto & Windus, 1996
Mellor, G.J. *Pom-poms and Ruffles*, Clapham, Dalesman Publishing Company, 1966
Parker, Larry. *But – what do you do in the winter?*, London, Concert Artistes' Association, 1996
Pertwee, Bill. *Beside the Seaside*, London, Collins & Brown, 1999

Pertwee, Bill. *Pertwee's Promenades and Pierrots*, Newton Abbott, David & Charles, 1979

Pulling, Christopher. *They Were Singing*, London, Harrap, 1952

Rose, Clarkson. *Beside the Seaside*, London, Museum Press, 1960

Rudlin, John. *Commedia dell'Arte an Actor's Handbook, op. cit.*

Stephen, Adrian. *The 'Dreadnought' Hoax*, Chatto & Windus, new edition 1983

Storey, Robert. *Pierrot A Critical History of a Mask*, Princeton, Princeton University Press, 1978

Taylor, John Russell. *Penguin Dictionary of the Theatre*, Harmondsworth, Penguin Books, 1966

Unpublished Sources

Minute Books of Weymouth Borough Council Amusement Committee, Dorset History Centre: WM/AD7/13 1903–1967

Recollections of Sheila Milton, Dawn Gould, Margaret Morris, Joyce Otter and Pamela Haines

CHAPTER THREE

Published Sources

ATTWOOLL 2, *op. cit.*

Burney, Fanny. *The Diary and Letters of Madame D'Arblay*, 1842

Carey, G.S. *Balnea*, second edition 1801

Chedzoy, Alan. *Seaside Weymouth*, Wimborne, Dovecote Press, 2003

Dickens, Charles (ed.) *Grimaldi the Clown*, London, George Routledge, Author's Edition 1884

Findlater, Richard. *Grimaldi King of Clowns*, London, Macgibbon & Kee, 1955

Gittings, Robert. *The Older Hardy*, London, Heinemann, 1978

Good, Ronald. *Weyland, op. cit.*

Hardy, Thomas. *A Changed Man*, London, Macmillan, 1913

Hardy, Thomas. *The Trumpet-Major*, London, Smith, Elder, & Co., 1880

Hare, Arnold. *The Georgian Theatre in Wessex*, London, Phoenix House, 1958

Hartnoll, Phyllis (ed.) *The Oxford Companion to the Theatre, op. cit.*

Hutchins, John. *The History and Antiquities of the County of Dorset*, first and second editions 1774, 1796–1815

Hibbert, Christopher, *George III*, London, Penguin, 1999

Hudd, Roy (ed.). *Dan Leno His Book*, London, Hugh Evelyn, 1968

Kay-Robinson, Denys. *The Landscape of Thomas Hardy*, Exeter, Webb & Bower,1984

Manvell, Roger. *Sarah Siddons Portrait of an Actress*, London, Heinemann, 1970

Millgate, Michael. *Thomas Hardy a Biography*, Oxford, Oxford University Press, 1982

New Weymouth Guide, Weymouth 1798

Southern, Richard. *The Georgian Playhouse*, London, Pleiades Books, 1948

Southern, Richard, and Brown, Ivor. *The Georgian Theatre, Richmond, Yorkshire*, Richmond, Georgian Theatre (Richmond) Trust, 1962

Taylor, Richard H. *The Personal Notebooks of Thomas Hardy*, London, Macmillan, 1975

Wilson, A.E. *The Story of Pantomime*, Wakefield, EP Publishing, reprint 1974

Adams, Victor. 'Weymouth Theatricals' in *Proceedings of the Dorset Natural History & Archaeological Society*, Vol. 89, 1965

Somerset & Dorset Notes and Queries, Vol. IX, Sherborne, 1905

Unpublished Sources

Collection of playbills for the Theatre Royal, Weymouth, Weymouth Reference Library

Papers of Victor Adams in Weymouth Reference Library

Playbills in the possession of Weymouth Museum

Notes on the theatre site by Stephen Mottram, 2007

Information from the Theatre Royal, Richmond, Yorks

CHAPTER FOUR

Published Sources

ATTWOOLL 1 & 2, *op. cit.*

Austen, Jane. *Emma*, 1816

Benson's New Weymouth Guide, Weymouth, B. Benson, 1831

Boyce, Benjamin. *The Benevolent Man, A Life of Ralph Allen of Bath*, Cambridge, Mass., Harvard University Press, 1967

Byng, John. *Rides Round Britain*, London, Folio Society, 1996

Chedzoy, Alan. *Seaside Weymouth, op. cit.*

Commins, J. *New Weymouth Guide*, 1829

Crane, John. *Cursory Notes on Sea-Bathing: the use of Sea-Water Internally, and the Advantages of a Maritime Situation, as condusing to Health & Longevity*, [c.1788]

Delamotte, Peter. *The Weymouth Guide*, Weymouth, Delamotte, third edition [1791]

Ellis, George Alfred. *History and Antiquities of Weymouth & Melcombe Regis*, Weymouth, B. Benson, 1829

Granville, A.B. *The Spas of England and Principal Sea-Bathing Places: Southern Spas*, 1841

Ham, Elizabeth (ed. Gillett, Eric). *Elizabeth Ham by Herself 1783–1820*, London, Faber & Faber, 1945

Hardy, Florence. *The Early Life of Thomas Hardy 1840–1891*, London, Macmillan, 1928

Hardy, Thomas. *The Mayor of Casterbridge*, London, Smith, Elder, & Co.,1886

Hardy, Thomas. *The Trumpet-Major, op. cit.*

[Harker, Jarvis]. *Sketches in, round, and about Weymouth* [1877]

Hutchins, John. *The History and Antiquities of the County of Dorset*, first edition, 1774

Marples, Morris. *White Horses and Other Hill Figures*, London, Country Life, 1949

Pindar, Peter (John Wolcot). 'The Royal Tour and Weymouth Amusements; a Solemn and Reprimanding Epistle to the Laureat', 1795

Smart, Hawley, *Broken Bounds*, [1874]
Treves, Frederick. *Highways and Byways in Dorset*, London, Macmillan, 1906

Dorset Yearbook 1985
Reeby, D.M.H. 'Weymouth's Spas – Nottington and Radipole' in *Proceedings of the Dorset Natural History and Archaeological Society*, Vol. 116, 1994
Scott, Edward. *Upwey Wishing Well*, undated pamphlet

Unpublished Sources

Broadley, A.M. *Royal Weymouth, 1789–1809*, vols 3 & 4. Ms. copy in Weymouth Reference Library. Also the source for extracts from William Holloway's ode of 1798
Correspondence and Papers concerning George III's Statue. Dorset History Centre: D/ASH:B/X3
Falkner, John Meade. 'Notes by John Meade Falkner 1859–71', *op. cit.*, D300/14
Lucking, J.H. 'Railways of Dorset', 1982. Thesis in Dorset County Museum
MacIntyre, Sylvia. 'Towns as Health and Pleasure Resorts: Bath, Scarborough and Weymouth 1700–1815, thesis 1973, in Weymouth Museum
Information supplied by John Willows, curator of Sutton Poyntz Water Museum.
Notes on Thomas Hardy and Weymouth by Stephen Mottram, 2007
www.users.globalnet.co.uk/~wykedh/webgeorge/chapfive.htm: an account of the architectural career of James Hamilton

CHAPTER FIVE

Published sources

ATTWOOLL 1 & 2, *op. cit.*

Chedzoy, Alan. *Seaside Weymouth, op. cit.*

Collier, John Payne (ed.). *Punch & Judy with Illustrations, op. cit.*

Ellis, George Alfred. *History and Antiquities of Weymouth & Melcombe Regis, op. cit.*

Falkner, John Meade. *Moonfleet,* 1898

Good, Ronald. *Weyland, op. cit.*

Ham, Elizabeth. *Elizabeth Ham by Herself, 1783-1820, op. cit.*

Hardy, Thomas *The Dynasts,* Parts l, ll and lll, London, Macmillan, 1903, 1905, 1908

Hardy, Thomas. *The Trumpet-Major, op. cit.*

Hardy, Thomas. *Wessex Poems.* London, Harper & Brothers, 1898

Morris, Stuart. *Portland an Illustrated History,* Wimborne, Dovecote Press, 1985

Poole, Steve. *The Politics of Regicide in England 1760–1850,* Manchester, Manchester University Press, 2000

Adams, Victor. 'Weymouth Theatricals', *op. cit.*

Unpublished Sources

Falkner, John Meade. 'Notes by John Meade Falkner 1859–71', *op. cit.,* D300/12 & 14

CHAPTER SIX

Published sources

Ackroyd, Peter. *London the Biography,* London, Chatto & Windus, 2000

Attwooll l and ll, *op. cit.*

Byrom, Michael. *Punch & Judy its origin and evolution, op. cit.*

Collier, John Payne (ed.). *Punch & Judy with Illustrations, op. cit.*

Dickens, Charles. *The Old Curiosity Shop*, London, 1841

Doré, Gustave & Jerrold, Blanchard. *London, a Pilgrimage*, London, Grant & Co., 1872

Gay, John. *The Beggar's Opera*, 1728

Guest, C. H. *Punch's Boy*, London, Hutchinson, 1942

Hall, Alice, 'Boys Together' in *Weymouth Memories*, Weymouth, Sherren [1897]

Hardy, Thomas. *The Mayor of Casterbridge*, op. cit.

[Harker, Jarvis]. *Sketches in, round, and about Weymouth*, op.cit.

Jackson, Arlene M. *Illustration and the Novels of Thomas Hardy*, London, Macmillan, 1982

Jeffery's Illustrated Weymouth Guide, Weymouth, [1858]

LEACH, *op. cit.*

Mayhew, Henry. *London Labour and the London Poor*, Vol. lll 1856

Purdy, Richard Little. *Thomas Hardy a Biographical Study*, Oxford, Oxford University Press, 1954

Rudlin, John. *Commedia dell'Arte an Actor's Handbook*, op. cit.

SPEAIGHT I & II, *op. cit.*

Stead, Philip John. *Mr. Punch*, op. cit.

Walton, John K. *The English Seaside Resort. A Social History 1750–1914*, Leicester, Leicester University Press, 1983

Woodensconce, Papernose [Robert Brough]. *The Wonderful Drama of Punch & Judy*, Bicester, DaSilva Puppet Books, 2001

Dorset Daily Echo, Feb 1 1955; April 9 and 21, 2004

Article on 'Guignol' in *Mon Journal*, undated

Oakley, M.R. 'A Survey on the Holiday Industry in England: Dorset', thesis, Oxford 1964, typescript in Weymouth Reference Library

Unpublished Sources

Railway exhibition in Weymouth Museum, Summer 2007

Information supplied by Guy Higgins

www.punchandjudy.com

www.punchandjudyfellowship.org.uk

CHAPTER SEVEN

Published sources

Felix, Geoff. (ed.). *Conversations with Punch*, Wembley Park, Middlesex, Geoff Felix, 1994

LEACH, *op. cit.*

Mayhew, Henry. *London Labour and the London Poor, op.cit.*

Pridham, Llewellyn, *The Dorset Coastline*, Dorchester, Longmans, [c.1955]

SPEAIGHT I & II, *op. cit.*

Wilkinson, Walter. *The Peep Show*, London, Geoffrey Bles, 1927

Wilkinson, Walter. *Puppets through Lancashire*, London, Geoffrey Bles, 1936

Wolff, Henry & West, Jack A.C. *Weymouth & Melcombe Regis in the Nineteenth Century*, Weymouth, Weymouth Central Library, 1972

Dorset Echo August 14 1959; July 14 1966; Fun Guide, June 1983; April 19 2000; April 21 2004; May 5 2005; August 5 2005

Leach, Robert. 'The Swatchel Omi: Punch and Judy and the Oral Tradition' in *Theatre Quarterly*, Vol. IX, Winter 1980

Western Gazette, August 21 2003

Unpublished Sources

Minute Books of Weymouth Borough Council Amusement Committee, *op. cit.*

Weymouth scrapbooks vols 1–18, Weymouth Reference Library, particularly those for 1922, 1923, 1924, 1925

Obituary of Guy Higgins by Mark Poulton, June 2007

Speech made by Mark Poulton at the unveiling of plaque to Guy Higgins, September 3 2007

Conversations with Professors Mark Poulton, Guy Higgins, Geoff Felix, Pete Maggs and Martin Bridle

Conversations with John Stockley, Pam Brady and Dawn Gould

Letters from Dawn Gould, Silvia Noakes and Bonny Sartin

CHAPTER EIGHT

Published sources

Byrom, Michael. *Punch & Judy its origin and evolution, op. cit.*
Collier, John Payne (ed.). *Punch & Judy with Illustrations, op. cit.*
Powys, John Cowper. *Weymouth Sands, op. cit.*
Stead, Philip John. *Mr. Punch, op. cit.*

Leach, Robert. 'The Swatchel Omi: Punch and Judy and the Oral Tradition' in *Theatre Quarterly, op. cit.*
Southern Times, Feb 22 1913; May 17 1913; June 28 1913; May 30 1914; June 6 1914
West Country Campers, May 30–June 6 1914 in Weymouth Reference Library
Western Gazette, August 21 2003

Unpublished Sources

Conversations with Rene Smith and Wendy Wharam

ENCORE ONE

Published sources

Braizer's House and Apartment Register, Weymouth, May 30 1868
Guide to the Weymouth Hotel n.d.
Robens, James Eaton. *Recollections of a Nonogenerian,* 1914
Kelly's Directories 1867, 1875, 1880, 1885, 1889, 1895, 1898, 1903, 1907, 1915, 1920, 1923, 1927, 1930–1
Visitors' Free Guide to Sunny Weymouth, 1904
Weymouth Visitors' Directory, Weymouth, D.Archer, 1854
*Weymouth Visitors' List,*1863

Unpublished sources

Georgina & Maxwell Grayson. Colin Ellis, Professor Malcolm Airs,
    Jane Penoyre, David Brown, Stephen Mottram
Engravings and photographs of Weymouth Esplanade in Weymouth
    Museum and Dorset County Museum

ENCORE TWO

Published sources

Wilkinson, Walter. *The Peep Show, op. cit.*
Wilkinson, Walter. *Vagabonds and Puppets*, London, Geoffrey Bles,
    1930

Wilkinson, Walter. 'First Puppet Show', *Puppetry Yearbook*, 1944
Article by Jonathan Glancey on Letchworth in the *Guardian*,
    December 1 2003

Unpublished Sources

'A Short History of an Amusing Enterprise: the Moonstruck
    Marionettes'. Three notebooks in Dorset County Museum

Index